Mind in Tibetan Buddhism

Mind in Tibetan Buddhism

Oral Commentary on
Ge-shay Jam-bel-sam-pel's
Presentation of Awareness and Knowledge
Composite of All the Important Points
Opener of the Eye of New Intelligence

Lati Rinbochay

TRANSLATED, EDITED, AND INTRODUCED
BY ELIZABETH NAPPER

Snow Lion Publications
Ithaca, New York USA

Snow Lion Publications
P.O. Box 6483
Ithaca, New York 14851
USA

First Published 1980
by Rider and Company, London

First Printing in USA 1980
Second Printing in USA 1981
Third Printing in USA 1986

Library of Congress Catalog Card Number 86-3799

ISBN 0-937938-02-5

Library of Congress Cataloging-in-Publication Data

Lati Rinbochay.
Mind in Tibetan Buddhism.

English and Tibetan
Bibliography: p.
Includes index.
1. 'Jam-dpal-bsam- 'phel. Blo rig gi rnam bzag ner mkho kun 'dus blo gsar mig 'byed.
2. Buddhism--Psychology. 3. Buddhism--China--Tibet--Doctrines. I. Napper, Elizabeth.
II. 'Jam-dpal-bsam- 'phel. Blo rig gi rnam bzag ner mkho kun 'dus blo gear mig 'byed.
III. Title.
BQ4570.P76L38 1986 128'.2 86-3799
ISBN 0-937938-02-5

Contents

Preface 7

PART ONE: *Introduction* 9

PART TWO: *Translation* 41

1 Consciousness 43

2 Direct Perceivers 49

3 Inferential and Subsequent Cognizers 75

4 Non-Cognizing Awarenesses 92

5 Division of Awareness and Knowledge into Three 111

6 Prime Cognizers 116

7 Other Twofold Divisions of Awareness and Knowledge 130

Glossary 147

Bibliography 155

Notes 161

Tibetan Text 167

Preface

Homage to Mañjushrī

Lati Rinbochay is a Tibetan lama of the Ge-luk (*dGe lugs*) order who was a Visiting Lecturer at the University of Virginia from March 1976 to May 1977 and is at present Abbot of the Shar-dzay College of Gan-den Monastery in Mundgod, South India. During the time he was at Virginia, he gave oral commentary on a contemporary Ge-luk-ba presentation of awareness and knowledge written by Ge-shay Jam-bel-sam-pel (dGe-bshes 'Jam-dpal-bsam-'phel, d. 1975).[1] This commentary was recorded, translated, and edited; interspersed with a translation of Ge-shay Jam-bel-sam-pel's text, it comprises Part Two of this book. Rich in detail found only in the oral tradition, it provides a basic orientation to Tibetan views on consciousness.

Part One is an introduction based on Lati Rinbochay's explanation as well as two other presentations of awareness and knowledge – one by Pur-bu-jok (Phur-bu-lcog Byams-pa-rgya-mtsho, 1825–1901), *Explanation of the Presentation of Objects and Object-Possessors as well as Awareness and Knowledge*,[2] and the other by Jam-yang-shay-ba ('Jam-dbyangs-bzhad-pa, 1648–1721), *A Presentation of Awareness and Knowledge*.[3] I received lengthy instruction on both of these from Lati Rinbochay and on the latter from Geshe Gedun Lodrö, Visiting Professor at the University of Virginia from January to August 1979.

The materials consulted for this work were exclusively Tibetan. However, inasmuch as Sanskrit terminology is more widely known than Tibetan, for key technical terms equivalents in both languages have been provided at their first occurrence. They can also be found in a glossary at the end, alphabetized according to the English. Those Sanskrit terms which may not actually have occurred in Sanskrit but are merely constructed based on the Tibetan are indicated by an asterisk. In transliterating Sanskrit *ch, sh,* and *ṣh* were used rather than *c, ṣ,* and *ś* for ease of pronunciation.

Titles of Indian and Tibetan texts are cited according to their English translation throughout; with the first occurrence of each Indian title, the Sanskrit is given. Also, throughout the text, both the author's name and the title of a work being cited are given, even though Lati Rinbochay or Ge-shay Jam-bel-sam-pel may have cited only one. The full Sanskrit and Tibetan titles can be found in the bibliography at the end, which is alphabetized according to the English translation. Tibetan names are given in an easily pronounceable form with citation of their transliteration according to the system devised by Turrell Wylie[4] with the exception that root rather than initial letters are capitalized.

It should be noted that throughout the text the terms 'conceptual consciousness', 'thought consciousness', and 'thought' have been used interchangeably to translate one Tibetan word *rtog pa* (Skt. *kalpanā*).

ELIZABETH NAPPER

PART ONE

Introduction

Awareness and knowledge (*blo-rig*) is the study of consciousness, of mind. Understanding mind is essential to understanding Buddhism in both its theoretical and practical aspects, for the process of achieving enlightenment is one of systematically purifying and enhancing the mind.

Mind and body, though associated, are not inseparably linked; they have different substantial causes. That this is so means that the increase and development of the mind is not limited to that of the body; though the continuum of the body ceases at death, that of the mind does not. This difference stems from the fact that whereas the body is composed of matter and as such is anatomically established, mind is not. It is an impermanent phenomenon (*anitya-dharma, mi rtag pa'i chos*), changing in each moment, and having a nature of clear light. Pure in its essential nature, the mind is stained by adventitious defilements (*ākasmika-mala, glo bur gyi dri ma*), the result of having misapprehended from beginningless time the actual nature of phenomena. These defilements can be removed; the mind can be totally purified, and the stages in this process of purification constitute the levels of progress towards enlightenment.

Within the Ge-luk-ba order of Tibetan Buddhism, on whose viewpoint this work is based, mind is first formally studied in the topic of 'Awareness and Knowledge'. It is the second major area of study undertaken during a course of intellectual training that culminates after twenty to twenty-five years of intensive study in the attainment of the degree of ge-shay (*dge bshes*).[5] 'Awareness and Knowledge' is primarily an identification of the different types of minds, of consciousnesses which occur in the mental continuum, an introduction to the vocabulary connected with the mind, and a means of training the student in the processes of reasoning – an endeavour integrally linked with all steps of the Ge-luk-ba ge-shay training. Consciousness is examined mainly by dividing it into types and subtypes from several points of view, whereby a student develops a sense of the variety of consciousnesses, their functions, and interrelationships. Not found within the topic of 'Awareness and Knowledge' are descriptions of means for developing and training the mind nor even of the stages in that process; these are included in such topics as 'Grounds and Paths', the 'Concentrations and Formless Absorptions', the 'Perfections', 'Madhyamaka', and so forth – later areas of study for which thorough familiarity with 'Awareness and Knowledge' provides a necessary basis.

Presentations of 'Awareness and Knowledge' find their primary source in the works of the great Indian commentators Dignāga (480–540) and Dharmakīrti (600–660),[6] especially in Dignāga's *Compendium on Prime Cognition* (*Pramāṇasamuchchaya*)[7] and in Dharmakīrti's *Seven Treatises on Prime Cognition*, particularly his *Commentary on (Dignāga's) 'Compendium on Prime Cognition'* (*Pramāṇavarttika*).[8] The one exception is the section on minds and mental factors (*chitta-chaitta, sems sems byung*) the source of which is Asaṅga's *Compendium of Knowledge* (*Abhidharmasamuchchaya*).[9]

These Indian texts as well as a number of Indian commentaries on them were translated into Tibetan, at the latest by the eleventh century[10] and the Tibetans continued the tradition of writing commentaries on them. They also began a new tradition of drawing important topics from those texts and presenting them in conjunction with the Sautrāntika mode of reasoning. The twelfth-century Ga-dam-ba (*bKa'-gdams-pa*) scholar Cha-ba-chö-gyi-seng-gay (Cha-pa-chos-kyi-seng-ge,

1109–1169) wrote the first text of this type, his work and subsequently the genre as a whole being entitled *The Collected Topics [of Prime Cognition]* (*bsDus sgrva*). His text, no longer extant, had eighteen sections, one of which was entitled 'A Presentation of Objects and Object-Possessors', a topic which includes within it what is studied as 'Awareness and Knowledge'.

Shortly after Cha-ba-chö-gyi-seng-gay, the Sa-gya (*Sa-skya*) scholar Sa-gya Pandita (Sa-skya Paṇḍita, 1182–1251/2) wrote a commentary on the Indian texts on prime cognition entitled *The Treasury of Reasoning.*[11] Contained within its second chapter is a complete presentation of 'Awareness and Knowledge'. Sa-gya Pandita himself wrote a commentary to this, and it was extensively elaborated on by later scholars within the Sa-gya tradition.

The founder of the Ge-luk-ba order, Tsong-ka-pa (Tsong-kha-pa, 1357–1419), did not write a separate presentation of 'Awareness and Knowledge' but did write a brief introductory commentary to Dharmakīrti's *Seven Treatises* entitled *Door of Entry to the Seven Treatises*;[12] this has three parts, the second of which, 'Object-Possessors', is a presentation of 'Awareness and Knowledge'. His disciple Kay-drup (mKhas-grub, 1385–1438) wrote a more extensive commentary on Dharmakīrti's *Seven Treatises, Clearing Away Darkness of Mind with Respect to the Seven Treatises,*[13] which includes a presentation of objects and object-possessors that extensively sets forth 'Awareness and Knowledge'. Another of Tsong-ka-pa's main disciples Gen-dun-drup (dGe-'dun-grub), the First Dalai Lama, 1391–1474) extensively set forth 'Awareness and Knowledge' within his *Ornament for Valid Reasoning.*[14]

The first Ge-luk-ba presentation of 'Awareness and Knowledge' as a separate text was probably that of Pan-chen Sö-nam-drak-ba (Paṇ-chen bSod-nams-grags-pa, 1478–1554),[15] textbook author for the Lo-sel-ling College of Dre-bung monastery. The next was that of Jam-yang-shay-ba, textbook author for the Go-mang College of Dre-bung, which is not so much a formal composition but his lectures on the topic to beginning students which were subsequently written down. The next was a very extensive presentation of 'Awareness and Knowledge' by Lo-sang-da-yang (bLo-bzang-rta-dbyangs, 1867–1937),[16] which is a composite of all those that preceded it. Another important and quite recent text of this type is Pur-bu-jok's *Explanation of the Presentation of Objects and Object-Possessors as well as Awareness and Knowledge* from within his *Presentation of the Collected Topics Revealing the Meaning of the Treatises on Prime Cognition*. The text by Ge-shay Jam-bel-sam-pel translated in Part Two of this book is a recent presentation of 'Awareness and Knowledge', written in Tibet sometime prior to 1959. The particular feature of this text, currently used by Lo-sel-ling College as its textbook for the study of 'Awareness and Knowledge' is that it is a very concise presentation of the topic which dispenses with the syllogistic format usually employed in such works and merely lays out directly the salient points concerning 'Awareness and Knowledge'.

The Tibetan presentations of 'Awareness and Knowledge' unquestionably derive from and rely on Indian sources. However, the Tibetans also contributed a great deal to the topic, both in systematizing it and in refining the use of terminology. Although all the various topics and divisions within 'Awareness and Knowledge' are considered by the Tibetans to be indicated in the Indian texts, in support of which sources can be cited, they are not always indicated with the terms by which they are known in Tibet. For example, among the sevenfold division of awareness and knowledge, only four – the first two and the last two (direct perceivers, inferential cognizers, doubt, and wrong consciousnesses) – are mentioned by name either by Dignāga or Dharmakīrti; the remaining three (subsequent cognizers, correctly assuming consciousnesses, and awarenesses to which the object appears but is not ascertained) are not explicitly mentioned, but that they are indicated is a necessary conclusion from the sources cited by Jam-yang-shay-ba. It appears that these terms were current in Tibet by the time of Sa-gya Pandita and perhaps even Cha-ba-chö-gyi-seng-gay,[17] but it is not clear whether they were an early Tibetan innovation or perhaps may be found in the later Sanskrit commentaries.[18] This is an excellent topic for future study, the goal of this work, however, being to set out clearly the basic Ge-luk-ba presentation of 'Awareness and Knowledge' in the context of the oral tradition.

Among the four systems of Buddhist tenets studied in Tibet – Vaibhāṣhika, Sautrāntika, Chittamātra, and Mādhyamika, in ascending order – the specific viewpoint of the study of 'Awareness and Knowledge' is Sautrāntika, and within the division of Sautrāntika into Followers of Scripture and Followers of Reasoning, the latter. However, the general presentation is common at least to Sautrāntika, Chittamātra and Mādhyamika, and thus a study of 'Awareness and Knowledge' is used as a basis for all areas of study, requiring only slight modifications for each area.

MIND AND ITS TYPES

Consciousness (*jñāna, shes pa*), awareness (*buddhi, blo*), and knower (*saṃvedana, rig pa*) are synonymous; they are the broadest terms among those dealing with the mind. Any mind (*chitta, sems*) or mental factor (*chaitta, sems byung*) is a consciousness, is an awareness, is a knower. These terms should be understood in an active sense because minds are momentary consciousnesses which are active agents of knowing. In Buddhism mind is not conceived to be merely a general reservoir of information or just the brain mechanism, but to be individual moments of knowing, the continuum of which makes up our sense of knowing.

Consciousnesses can be divided in a number of different ways; a major mode of division is into seven:

I. SEVENFOLD DIVISION

1 direct perceivers (*pratyakṣha, mngon sum*)
2 inferential cognizers (*anumāṇa, rjes dpag*)
3 subsequent cognizers (**parichchhinna-jñana, bcad shes*)[19]

4 correctly assuming consciousnesses (**manaḥ parīkṣhā, yid dpyod*)
5 awarenesses to which the object appears but is not ascertained (**aniyata-pratibhāsa, snang la ma nges pa*)
6 doubting consciousnesses (*saṃshaya, the tshom*)
7 wrong consciousnesses (*viparyaya-jñāna, log shes*)

Direct perceivers

Direct perceivers are, by definition, knowers which are free from conceptuality (*kalpanā-apodha, rtog bral*) and non-mistaken (*abhrānta, ma 'khrul ba*). To be free from conceptuality means that such a consciousness deals with its object directly without making use of an internal image. This is illustrated by the difference between seeing a pot – as is done by a directly perceiving sense consciousness – and thinking about a pot – as is done by a conceptual mental consciousness. In the first case, the consciousness is produced in dependence on contact with an actual pot, whereas in the second the mind is dealing only with a mental image of a pot.

To be non-mistaken means that there is no erroneous element involved in that which is appearing to the consciousness. As will be explained below (page 21), conceptual consciousnesses are necessarily mistaken in this regard; thus, the qualification 'non-mistaken' alone would be sufficient to eliminate them from the category of direct perceivers. 'Free from conceptuality', though redundant, is specifically stated in order to eliminate the non-Buddhist Vaisheṣhika view that there are conceptual sense consciousnesses.

The term 'non-mistaken' also eliminates from the class of direct perceivers those non-conceptual (*nirvikalpaka, rtog med*) consciousnesses which are mistaken due to a superficial cause of error (**pratibhāṣhikī-bhrānti-hetm, phral gyi 'khrul rgyu*)[20] such as a fault in the eye, sickness, and so forth. These are free from conceptuality, but not from mistake. An example is an eye consciousness of someone riding in a boat, to whom the trees on the shore appear to be moving. That person's eye consciousness is non-conceptual, for it is dealing directly with the trees, but is mistaken with respect to them in that they appear to be moving whereas they are not; thus, such a consciousness is not a direct perceiver.

Direct perceivers are of four types:

1 sense direct perceivers (*indriya-pratyakṣha, dbang po'i mngon sum*)
2 mental direct perceivers (*mānasa-pratyakṣha, yid kyi mngon sum*)
3 self-knowing direct perceivers (*svasaṃvedana-pratyakṣha, rang rig mngon sum*)
4 yogic direct perceivers (*yogi-pratyakṣha, rnal 'byor mngon sum*)

Sense direct perceivers are of five types: those apprehending forms (*rūpa, gzugs*), sounds (*shabda, sgra*), odours (*gandha, dri*), tastes (*rasa, ro*), and tangible objects (*spraṣhṭavya, reg bya*). They are produced upon the aggregation of three conditions:

1 observed object condition (*ālambana-pratyaya, dmigs rkyen*)
2 uncommon empowering condition (*asādhāraṇa-adhipati-pratyaya, thun mong ma yin pa'i bdag rkyen*)
3 immediately preceding condition (*samanantara-pratyaya, de ma thag rkyen*)

Using the example of an eye consciousness (*chakṣhur-vijñāna, mig gi rnam shes*)[21] its observed object condition is the form it perceives. Its uncommon empowering condition is the eye sense power (*chakṣhur-indriya, mig dbang*), a type of clear internal matter which empowers it in the sense that it enables it to comprehend visible forms as opposed to sounds, tastes, and so forth. Its immediately preceding condition is a moment of consciousness which occurs immediately before it and makes it an experiencing entity.

In all systems but Vaibhāṣhika, cause and effect must occur in a temporal sequence – they cannot be simultaneous. Thus, since the object observed by a consciousness is one of its causes, it must precede that consciousness, and therefore a consciousness is posited as knowing a phenomenon which exists one moment before it. Moreover, although consciousnesses are momentary phenomena, that is, disintegrate moment by moment, one moment of consciousness is too brief to be noticed by ordinary persons. Rather, what we experience as sense perception is a continuum of moments of consciousness apprehending a continuum of moments of an object which is also disintegrating moment by moment.

Sense direct perceivers do not name their objects nor reflect on them. Non-conceptual in nature, they merely experience. All discursive thought about the object observed by sense direct perception is done by later moments of conceptual consciousness induced by that sense perception. Within the Buddhist tradition this has caused sense direct perceivers to be labelled 'stupid' and has led to the widespread view among Western interpreters of Buddhism that sense consciousnesses are mere passive 'transmitters', passing a signal from the sense organ to thought. Such is not the case, for sense consciousnesses do *know*, do realize (*adhigam, rtogs*) their object. Not only that, but sense consciousnesses can also be trained such that an eye consciousness can know not only that a person being seen is a man but also that that person is one's father. This is not to say that the eye consciousness labels the person, 'This is my father,' but it does know it, and that knowledge induces the subsequent conceptual consciousness which actually affixes the name 'father' without any intervening reflection. Sense consciousnesses are also capable of comprehending their object's ability to perform a function; thus, an eye consciousness itself can perceive that fire has the capacity to cook and burn.

The second division of direct perceivers, mental direct perceivers, has two types. The Ge-luk-bas assert that at the end of a continuum of sense direct perception of an object there is generated one moment of mental direct perception; this in turn induces conceptual cognition of that object, naming it and so forth. That one moment at the end of sense direct perception is the first type of mental direct perception. It is too brief to be noticed by ordinary beings but can be observed by Superiors (*Ārya, 'Phags pa*) those advanced in meditative training who have through extensive practice developed the ability to perceive selflessness directly. The second type of mental direct perception includes various types of clairvoyances (*abhijñā, mngon shes*) such as the ability to know others' minds, to remember one's former lives, to perceive forms and sounds too distant or subtle to be apprehended by the sense consciousnesses, and so forth.

The third type of direct perceiver is a self-knower. The positing or not of the existence of such a direct perceiver serves as a major basis for distinguishing schools of tenets; among the four tenet systems – Vaibhāṣhika, Sautrāntika, Chittamātra, and Mādhyamika – Sautrāntika, Chittamātra, and Yogāchāra-Svātantrika-Mādhyamika posit the existence of self-knowers, whereas Vaibhāṣhika, Sautrāntika-Svātantrika-Mādhyamika and Prāsaṅgika-Mādhyamika deny the existence of such. For those schools which do posit the existence of a self-knower, its function is to make possible the memory of one's cognitions. Its proponents say that if there were no consciousness observing the consciousness that perceives an object, there would be no way for one to know that one had perceived something. The systems which do not assert self-knowers deny that they are necessary in order to remember one's cognitions and say that positing them leads to an infinite regress of self-knowers knowing the self-knowers, and so forth.

The function of a self-knower is just to make possible memory of former consciousnesses. It does not have an active role of introspection, or self-awareness, as its name might suggest; such is carried out by a mental factor called introspection (*samprajanya, shes bzhin*) which can accompany a main consciousness. Thus, self-knowers are not something which one seeks to develop as part of training the mind. They perform their function in the same way at all levels of mental development.

The fourth and final type of direct perceiver is a yogic direct perceiver. Unlike clairvoyances which can occur in the continuum of anyone – Buddhist or non-Buddhist – and do not necessarily require advanced mental training, yogic direct perceivers occur only in the continuums of Superiors, that is, those who from among the five paths – accumulation (*sambhāra-mārga, tshogs lam*), preparation (*prayoga-mārga, sbyor lam*), seeing (*darshana-mārga, mthong lam*), meditation (*bhāvanā-mārga, sgom lam*), and no more learning (*ahaikṣha-mārga, mi slob lam*) – have attained the path of seeing or above. Whereas the uncommon empowering condition of the five sense direct perceivers is their respective sense power, such as that of the eye, ear, nose, and so forth, the uncommon empowering condition of yogic direct perceivers is a meditative stabilization (*samādhi, ting nge 'dzin*) which is a union of calm abiding (*shamatha, zhi gnas*) and special insight (*vipashyanā, lhag mthong*). Thus, yogic direct perceivers are a level of consciousness very different from ordinary sense perception despite their similarity in being non-mistaken, non-conceptual knowers of objects.

The development of yogic direct perceivers is a major goal of meditative training. Although one effortlessly has the capacity to perceive directly such things as forms and sounds with an eye or ear consciousness, one does not have that ability with regard to profound phenomena such as subtle impermanence and selflessness. Thus, these must originally be understood conceptually, that is, they are comprehended by way of a mental image rather than directly. Then, through repeated familiarization with the object realized, it is possible to develop clearer and clearer realization until finally the need for a mental image is transcended and one realizes the object directly. Such yogic direct perceivers have great force, being able to overcome the misconceptions that bind one in cyclic existence.

Direct perceivers, therefore, include both ordinary and highly developed consciousnesses.

Inferential cognizers

An inferential cognizer is a type of conceptual consciousness which realizes, or incontrovertibly gets at, an object of comprehension which cannot be initially realized by direct perception. Generated as the culmination of a process of reasoning, it is said to be produced in dependence on a correct sign (*liṅga, rtags*) acting as its basis. The meaning of this can be illustrated with a worldly example; if one looks out the window and sees smoke billowing from a neighbouring house, one will immediately infer that inside the house there is fire. The basis, the sign in dependence on which this inference was generated, was the presence of smoke. Because of the fact that there is an invariable relationship between the presence of an effect – in this case smoke – and the preceding existence of its cause – fire, one can correctly infer that fire is present. Such knowledge is not direct perception, for one did not actually see the fire; nonetheless it is valid, reliable knowledge.

Inasmuch as an inferential cognizer incontrovertibly realizes its object of cognition it is as reliable a form of knowledge as is a direct perceiver. However, there is the difference that whereas a direct perceiver contacts its object directly and non-mistakenly, an inferential cognizer, being conceptual, must get at its object through the medium of an image. That image, called a meaning generality (*artha-sāmānya, don spyi*), appears to thought as if it were the actual object although it is not, and in this respect a conceptual consciousness is mistaken with respect to the object that is appearing to it. This element of error does not, however, interfere with the accuracy with which that consciousness comprehends the object represented by the meaning generality, and thus it is a correct and incontrovertible (*avisaṃvādin, mi slu ba*) knower.

All conceptual consciousnesses are mistaken with respect to the object that appears to them, the meaning generality, and thus all are said to be mistaken consciousnesses (*bhrānti-jñāna, 'khrul shes*). However, only some are mistaken with respect to the actual object they are comprehending, the object in which thought is actually engaged. Conceptual consciousnesses which are not mistaken with respect to the object they are getting at are mistaken consciousnesses, but not wrong consciousnesses; those mistaken with respect to the object being gotten at are also wrong consciousnesses. Inferential cognizers are, by definition, *not* mistaken with respect to the object comprehended, being incontrovertible in the sense that their realization is firm; this gives them their force and validity.

Subsequent cognizers

The first moment of a direct perceiver comprehends its object through the force of experience; the first moment of an inference does so in dependence on a sign. For both those types of perception, later moments within the same continuum of perception, that is, while still apprehending the same object, no longer rely on either experience or a sign but are merely induced through the force of the first moment of cognition. These later moments are called subsequent cognizers. The strength of the initial realization has not been lost, and therefore subsequent cognizers are incontrovertible knowers that do realize their objects. However, the element of realization is not gained through their own power, for they themselves do not do the removing of superimpositions (*āropa, sgro 'dogs*) which enables realization to occur. Rather, they realize that which has already been realized by the former moment of consciousness which has already removed superimposition and which induces them.

Correctly assuming consciousnesses

A correctly assuming consciousness is, as the translation indicates, necessarily a correct mode of thought; it must also be a conceptual consciousness as opposed to direct cognition. What distinguishes it from the above three types of consciousnesses – direct perceivers, inferential cognizers, and subsequent cognizers – is that unlike them it does not realize its object; it is not incontrovertible. Thus, a distinction is made between merely being correct with regard to an object and actually realizing, or getting at, that object. The reason for this difference lies in the mode of generation; whereas, firstly, direct perception is generated through the force of experience, secondly, an inferential cognizer is generated as the culmination of a lengthy and convincing process of reasoning, and, thirdly, subsequent cognizers are continuations of direct perceivers or inferential consciousnesses, correctly assuming consciousnesses arrive at their conclusions either without reason, in a manner contrary to correct reasoning, or based on correct reasoning but without bringing it to its full conclusion. Most of the information we take in by listening to teachers or reading books, etc., falls within the category of correct assumption; much is just accepted, and even most which we think about and analyse has not been realized with the full force of inference. Because of the weakness of the basis from which it is generated, a correctly assuming consciousness is not a reliable form of knowledge as it lacks incontrovertibility; one will easily lose the force of one's conviction, as, for example, when confronted by someone strongly presenting an opposite viewpoint.

Awarenesses to which the object appears but is not ascertained

An awareness to which an object appears but is not ascertained is a type of direct perceiver, set forth separately within the sevenfold division of awarenesses and knowers to emphasize that not all direct perceivers are minds which realize their objects. Like direct perceivers, they are non-conceptual consciousnesses which are non-mistaken with respect to the object they are comprehending. However, these are minds which for some reason, such as one's attention being intently directed elsewhere or the duration of the consciousness being too brief to be noticed, are unable subsequently to induce ascertainment (*nishchaya, nges pa*) knowing that one had that particular perception. A familiar example of this occurs when one is walking down a street while intently engaged in conversation with someone and has a sense of people passing by but later cannot at all identify who they were. Such a mind is not mistaken, for in that it does not perceive something that is not actually so to be so, it has not introduced an element of error; thus it is included among direct perceivers. However, because it does not provide reliable information and has no factor of certainty, it is not considered to realize its object or to be incontrovertible.

Doubting consciousnesses

Necessarily conceptual in nature, doubting consciousnesses are minds distinguished primarily by their quality of indecisiveness, or two-pointedness. Doubt can tend towards one side of an issue or another, or it can be completely undecided, but it is always accompanied by an element of uncertainty. The most forceful conclusion doubt can arrive at is, 'Probably it is such and such.' Included within doubt are consciousnesses that are correct, incorrect, and those that are neither. For example, a mind which wonders whether or not future lives exist and thinks that probably they do would be doubt tending toward the fact (*don 'gyur gyi the tshom*), correct doubt; one which wonders whether or not they exist and thinks that probably they do not would be doubt not tending to the fact (*don mi 'gyur gyi the tshom*), or incorrect; and one which merely wondered whether or not future lives exist and entertained both positions equally would be equal doubt (*cha mnyam pa'i the tshom*), neither correct nor incorrect.

Although inferior in force of realization to even correct assumption and far from the incontrovertibility of direct perception and inference, doubt tending toward the fact is nonetheless a powerful initial step in weakening the force of a strongly adhered to wrong view and in beginning the process toward development of correct understanding.

Emphasizing the force of doubt tending to the fact, Āryadeva's *Four Hundred* says, 'Those whose merit is small have no doubts about this doctrine [the profound nature of phenomena]. Even through merely having doubts, cyclic existence is torn to tatters.'[22]

Wrong consciousnesses

Wrong consciousnesses are those that are mistaken with respect to the object they are engaged in, the object which is actually being comprehended. As such they are to be distinguished from mistaken consciousnesses which, as described above in the context of inference, are mistaken with respect to what appears to them. For example, conceptual consciousnesses are mistaken in that an image of the object appears to them as the actual object, but nonetheless they are capable of realizing correctly their object of comprehension. Such is not the case with wrong consciousnesses which cannot realize their objects and are thoroughly mistaken with respect to them.

Wrong consciousnesses are of two types, non-conceptual and conceptual. Non-conceptual ones are, for instance, an eye consciousness which sees snow-covered mountains as blue, an eye consciousness which due to jaundice sees everything as yellow, an eye consciousness which sees a double moon, and so forth. Because what appears to a non-conceptual consciousness is just the object that it is comprehending, or engaged in, a consciousness mistaken with respect to its appearing object (**pratibhāsa-viṣhaya, snang yul*) is necessarily mistaken with respect to its object of engagement (**pravṛtti-viṣhaya, 'jug yul*) and thus, non-conceptual wrong consciousnesses are mistaken with respect to both.

Wrong conceptual consciousnesses are, for instance, a mind which conceives that there are no former or future lives or one which conceives that there is a substantially existent self (*dravya-sat-ātman, rdzas yod kyi bdag*). Being conceptual, these minds are necessarily mistaken with respect to their appearing object – an image of that being comprehended which mistakenly appears to be the actual object. In addition they are mistaken with respect to the object being engaged in, thinking in the case of the view of the non-existence of former and future lives that what does exist does not and in the case of the view of self that what does not exist does.

These conceptual wrong consciousnesses provide the *raison d'être* for Buddhist meditational practice, for what Buddhism posits as the root cause, the basic motivating antecedent, of the endless round of birth, ageing, sickness, and death in which beings powerlessly cycle and in limitless ways suffer is just a wrong consciousness – the misapprehension of self where there is none. The way to free oneself from this suffering, to attain liberation from cyclic existence, is to identify its root as this misapprehension of self and then engage in a means to overcome it. The means identified by the Ge-luk-ba tradition is reasoning (*nyāya, rigs pa*), and one can take the sevenfold division of awareness and knowledge as illustrative of the stages one might go through while developing correct understanding through its use.

One begins with a wrong view such as the idea that there is a substantially existent self. As long as this idea is held forcefully, it is a wrong consciousness. Then, through hearing teachings of selflessness one might begin to wonder whether in fact there is such a self. At this point one would have generated doubt; initially one's tendency could still be to think that most likely there was a self – this would be doubt not tending to the fact. Through repeated thought one would pass through the stage of equal doubt in which, wondering whether or not there is a substantially existent self, one reaches no conclusion either way, and would eventually develop doubt tending to the fact in which one feels that there probably is no self but is nonetheless still uncertain.

The next step in the development of the view of selflessness is to generate a correctly assuming consciousness, one which definitely decides that there is no substantially existent self. At this point one is holding the correct view. However, one has not yet realized selflessness, although the oral tradition describes the initial generation of correct assumption with regard to selflessness as a very powerful experience. It is now necessary to contemplate selflessness again and again, using reasoning, seeking to develop a certainty from which one cannot be shaken.

An inference is the end result of a specific process of reasoning. One establishes that if there were a substantially existent self, it would have to exist in one of a limited number of ways and that if it does not exist in any of those ways, it does not exist; through reasoned investigation one establishes that it does not exist in any of those ways and hence concludes that it does not exist. For this conclusion to have the force of reasoned conviction, one must go through the steps of this investigation over and over again, so that one is accustomed to it and thoroughly convinced of it. One's consciousnesses throughout this process of familiarization are correct assumptions; when this is brought to the point of unwavering certainty, one generates an inference.

With the generation of an inferential cognizer, one can be said to have realized selflessness and to have incontrovertible knowledge of it. However, this is not the end of the process, for at this point one's realization is still conceptual, is still getting at selflessness only by way of an image. The goal is to develop one's realization still more and to bring it finally to the point of direct perception in which all need for an image has disappeared and one's mental consciousness is able to contact its object directly; such direct perception of selflessness is the actual antidote which, upon extended cultivation, is able to eradicate for ever the conception of self as well as all the other wrong views and afflictions that conception brings with it, thereby making liberation from cyclic existence possible.

The way in which an inference is transformed into direct perception is just repeated familiarization with the object of meditation. One's initial inference was generated in dependence on a sign. Later moments of that realization are subsequent cognizers, no longer directly dependent on the reasoning. Through taking selflessness to mind again and again within the force of one's realization, the clarity of appearance gradually increases until finally the image of the object disappears and is replaced by just clear appearance of the object itself. When this occurs, one has generated direct perception of one's object of meditation. This initial direct perception of selflessness is able to eradicate completely and forever a portion of the apprehension of self, but is not able to get rid of all levels of that conception. Inasmuch as the conception of self is the root of cyclic existence – is that view which has bound countless beings in immeasurable suffering since beginningless time – it is deeply ingrained and its force is extremely great. Initial direct perception overcomes only the grossest level of it, those conceptions based on false reasoning and so forth. One must then continue to cultivate realization of selflessness, developing the force of one's direct perception; direct perceivers of increasing strength overcome more and more subtle levels of the conception of self until finally it is eradicated completely.

The sevenfold division of awareness and knowledge is not an exhaustive presentation of consciousness – there are minds not included anywhere within it, such as highly developed conceptual meditative consciousnesses like great compassion and non-conceptual ones in which a yogi views all his surroundings as only earth or only water.[23] Rather, the sevenfold division is a distinguishing of various types of consciousness in terms of their correctness and incorrectness and the degree to which they actually get at their objects, as well as an ordering of them in terms of preference.

II. THREEFOLD DIVISION

The division of awarenesses and knowers into three is in terms of the object appearing to them. The three are:

1 conceptual consciousnesses which take a meaning generality as their apprehended object
2 non-conceptual non-mistaken consciousnesses which take a specifically characterized phenomenon as their apprehended object
3 non-conceptual mistaken consciousnesses which take a clearly appearing non-existent as their apprehended object.

There are four main types of object posited for consciousnesses:

1 object of engagement (**pravṛtti-viṣhaya, 'jug yul*)
2 determined object (**adhyavasāya-viṣhaya, zhen yul*)
3 appearing object (**pratibhāsa-viṣhaya, snang yul*)
4 apprehended object (*grāhya-viṣhaya, bzung yul*)[24]

The first two refer to the object that a consciousness is actually getting at and understanding. However, there is the qualification that the term 'determined object' is used only for conceptual consciousnesses, whereas 'object of engagement' is used for both conceptual and non-conceptual consciousnesses. Thus the object of engagement of an eye consciousness apprehending blue is blue; both the object of engagement and the determined object of a *thought* consciousness thinking about blue are blue.

The latter two types of objects – appearing and apprehended – refer to the object which is actually appearing to the conciousness and not necessarily to what it is comprehending. Since the actual object that appears to direct perception is what it realizes, its appearing object, apprehended object, and object of engagement are all the same – in the example of an eye consciousness apprehending blue, all three are blue. However, for a conceptual consciousness, although the object of engagement and determined object are the actual object the consciousness is understanding – i.e., blue for a thought consciousness apprehending blue – the appearing object and apprehended object are just an image of blue, called a meaning generality.

This threefold division of consciousnesses centres on differences in the appearing, or apprehended, objects of different types of consciousnesses. All thought consciousnesses necessarily take as their appearing object a meaning generality. A meaning generality is a permanent phenomenon in that it does not disintegrate moment by moment as do impermanent phenomena and it is a negative phenomenon, an image which is a mere elimination of all that is not the object. Thus, for example, the meaning generality of pot that appears to a thought consciousness apprehending pot is not an externally existent pot with all its own uncommon features, but just a general image 'pot' which is described negatively as being an appearance of the opposite of that which is not pot. The relative impoverishment of such an image in comparison to the richness of the appearance of the object involved in direct perception is the reason why direct perception is so much more highly valued than thought. However, in order to understand things which we are now unable to perceive directly, we must rely on thought, for it provides the means to train the mind so that direct perception can eventually be developed. Thus, in this system although thought is finally transcended by direct perception, its importance as the means to that goal is recognized and valued.

It is a common Western misunderstanding of Buddhism that because external objects cannot appear directly to thought but must be realized by means of an image, thought has absolutely no relationship to objects. This fails to take into account the two types of objects of thought consciousnesses; although that which appears to thought – for example, an appearance of the elimination of all that is not pot – is indeed only an image and not the actual object, the determined object of that consciousness, that which is understood through the image, is just that object itself. What it causes one to understand is just pot and not anything else such as house. The negative nature of the image eliminates everything else and leaves as that to be realized just pot. Thus, thought is a reliable way to ascertain objects.

The last two of the threefold division of awareness and knowledge are made from the viewpoint of the objects apprehended by non-conceptual consciousnesses. The first is a non-conceptual non-mistaken knower which takes as its apprehended object a specifically characterized phenomenon (*svalakṣhaṇa, rang mtshan*). It is synonymous with direct perceiver. Here, the emphasis is on the object appearing to such a consciousness – a specifically characterized phenomenon, synonymous in the Sautrāntika system with an impermanent phenomenon. Any impermanent phenomenon is suitable to be the appearing object of a direct perceiver, but no permanent phenomenon can, as the permanent appear only to thought.

The use of the term 'specifically characterized phenomenon' emphasizes that, unlike permanent phenomena which are mere imputations by thought, impermanent things have their own uncommon, or specific, characteristics which can appear to a direct perceiver. For example, whereas the image of pot that appears to thought is general in that it serves to represent all pots at different times in different places, a specifically characterized pot is unique – of a certain size, shape, colour, in a certain place, at a certain time. Furthermore, all the uncommon characteristics of a pot appear to the direct perceiver that apprehends it. In the Sautrāntika system all the qualities that are established, abide, and cease with a thing – such as its shape, colour, impermanence, nature of being a product, and so forth – appear to any direct perceiver apprehending that object. An ordinary direct perceiver is unable to *notice* all of these, but a yogic direct perceiver can see and ascertain them.

Because the clarity of perception of the object is so much greater for direct perceivers than for conceptual consciousnesses the former are said to have clear appearance (*spuṭābha, gsal snang*) of their object whereas the latter do not. The third of the threefold division, non-conceptual mistaken consciousnesses, are also said to have clear appearance because they perceive their objects without relying on an image. However, in their case what appears is a non-existent rather than a specifically characterized phenomenon. For example, one might clearly see blue snow mountains, but blue snow mountains do not exist. Such a consciousness is mistaken in that a clearly appearing non-existent is seen as if it did exist.

III. TWOFOLD DIVISIONS

There are many twofold divisions of awareness and knowledge, of which six are discussed in the text translated here, each approaching the subject of consciousness from a slightly different angle.

Prime cognizers and non-prime consciousnesses

A prime cognizer (*pramāṇa, tshad ma*) is defined as a knower which is new and incontrovertible.[25] From within the sevenfold division of awarenesses and knowers, the first three – direct perceivers, inferential cognizers, and subsequent cognizers – are necessarily incontrovertible. However, only some direct perceivers and inferential cognizers and no subsequent cognizers fulfil the second qualification of a prime cognizer –

newness. Only the first moment of a continuum of consciousness apprehending an object is considered new.

Thus, the first moment of a direct perceiver is a direct prime cognizer (*pratyakṣha-pramāṇa, mngon sum tshad ma*), for it is both new and incontrovertible; later moments within the same continuum – i.e., knowing the same object and without interruption by a consciousness knowing another object – are still direct perceivers but, no longer prime cognizers, are now subsequent cognizers. Similarly the first moment of an inferential cognizer is an inferential prime cognizer (*anumāna-pramāṇa, rjes dpag tshad ma*) whereas later moments within the same continuum of consciousness are inferential subsequent cognizers.[26] Thus from within the sevenfold division of awareness and knowledge, only the first moments of direct perceivers and inferential cognizers are prime cognizers; all later moments of these two as well as all instances of the other five types of consciousnesses – subsequent cognizers, correctly assuming consciousnesses, awarenesses to which the object appears but is not ascertained, doubting consciousnesses and wrong consciousnesses – are non-prime consciousnesses (*apramāṇa-jñāna, tshad min gyi shes pa*).

The division into prime and non-prime consciousnesses is an exhaustive one for any specific consciousness is one or the other.[27] Limiting the types of prime cognition to two in this way is specifically done to set the Buddhist view off from that of various non-Buddhist systems, which accept many other sources of prime, or valid, cognition such as the Vedas, example, and so forth. The Buddhist assertion is that two types of prime cognizers are both sufficient and exhaustive.

Conceptual and non-conceptual consciousnesses

This again is an exhaustive division of awarenesses and knowers, the emphasis here being on the manner in which a consciousness gets at its object – either directly or by means of an image. No statement is made as to relative correctness or newness, for included within each are both right and wrong as well as prime and non-prime consciousnesses.

Mistaken and non-mistaken consciousnesses

This division is made in terms of the correctness or incorrectness of consciousnesses with respect to what appears to them – their appearing or apprehended object – as opposed to their object of engagement. Thus, non-mistaken consciousness is a category which includes only correct non-conceptual consciousnesses – i.e., direct perceivers. All conceptual consciousnesses are included within mistaken consciousnesses inasmuch as the image of the object they are comprehending appears to them to be the actual object. A wrong conceptual consciousness such as one conceiving sound to be permanent and a right one conceiving the opposite are both mistaken with respect to their appearing objects, and thus both are classed as mistaken consciousnesses.

The appearing object and object of engagement of *non-conceptual* wrong consciousnesses are the same thing; thus, once such a consciousness is mistaken with respect to its object of engagement, it is also necessarily mistaken with respect to its appearing object whereby it is both a wrong and a mistaken consciousness.

Mental and sense consciousnesses

Again an exhaustive division, these consciousnesses are described in terms of whether the knower of an object is one of the five sense consciousnesses (*indriya-jñāna, dbang shes*) – eye, ear, nose, tongue, or body – or is a mental consciousness (*mano-vijñāna, yid kyi rnam shes*). The difference is one of basis (*āshraya, rten*). Sense consciousnesses are produced in dependence upon an uncommon empowering condition which is a physical sense power – eye, ear, nose, tongue, or body sense power – which is clear matter located within the sense organ – eye, ear, nose, tongue, and throughout the body; mental consciousnesses are produced in dependence on a mental sense power – a former moment of consciousness.

Sense consciousnesses are necessarily non-conceptual; mental consciousnesses can be either conceptual or non-conceptual.

Mental, self-knowing, and yogic direct perceivers are all non-conceptual mental consciousnesses. Inference, correct assumption, doubt, and so forth are conceptual mental consciousnesses. A conceptual consciousness is necessarily a mental and not a sense consciousness.

Eliminative and collective engagers

This division, again exhaustive, resembles the division into conceptual and non-conceptual consciousnesses and like it is a way of describing how a consciousness gets at its object. All conceptual consciousnesses are eliminative engagers (**apoha-pravṛtti, sel 'jug*); all non-conceptual ones are collective engagers (**vidhi-pravṛtti, sgrub 'jug*). Whereas in the conceptual/non-conceptual division the emphasis is on what the consciousness sees, i.e., whether the actual object or an image of the object appears to it, here the emphasis is on the way in which that consciousness apprehends its object.

A direct perceiver is a collective engager in the sense that all the factors of its object – all those things that are established with the object, abide with it, and disintegrate when it does – such as the individual particles of the object, its impermanence, momentariness, and so forth, appear to that consciousness.[28] It engages its object in a positive manner, without eliminating anything. However, the mere appearance of all these to the consciousness does not mean that they are necessarily ascertained; most are not noticed due to the interference of thought and predispositions. For example, when an ordinary person sees a pot, its momentary impermanence is not noticed due to the force of thick predispositions for apprehending permanence and due to seeing the conjunction of former and later moments of similar type. However, with training, one can come eventually to notice all these factors that appear to direct perception.

Thought on the other hand engages its object in an eliminative manner. Not apprehending all the uncommon features of an object, thought apprehends a general image which is a mere elimination; thus, a thought apprehending pot sees an image which is the opposite of that which is non-pot. Thought lacks precision – golden pot, copper pot, silver pot and so forth are all seen as 'pot', their shared quality of 'potness' taking precedence over their many dissimilar features. Also thought mixes time, as, for example, when one sees someone and thinks, 'This is the person I saw yesterday.' Because thought operates in a negative, or eliminative, manner it can never come to perceive all the uncommon features of its object as can direct perception, and this is why this system values direct perception so much more than thought. However, this does not make thought worthless or something to be immediately and utterly abandoned, for thought is the means by which direct perception can be trained to ascertain all those things which now appear to it but are not noticed. Left just as it is, direct perception would not naturally improve; however, careful use of thought such as training in the processes of reasoning, can gradually bring direct perception to its full potential in Buddhahood. At such a time thought is no longer necessary, but prior to that point there is no way of progressing without the use of thought.

Minds and mental factors

This twofold division is a way of describing the various functions of consciousness. Mind (*chitta, sems*) here is synonymous with main mind (*gtso sems*) and is that which knows the mere entity of the object being apprehended. Minds are accompanied by mental factors which apprehend various features of that object, affecting the manner in which the mind apprehends its object and so forth. Minds and mental factors have, with respect to any particular object, five similarities (*samprayukta, mtshungs par ldan pa*):

1 They are produced in dependence on the same basis (*āshraya, rten*), and thus if the eye sense power is the uncommon empowering condition of the main mind it is also that of the accompanying mental factors
2 they observe the same object (*ālambana, dmigs pa*)

3 they are generated in the same aspect (*ākāra, rnam pa*), in that if the eye consciousness is generated in the aspect of blue, the accompanying mental factors are also generated in the aspect of blue
4 they occur at the same time (*kālā, dus*), in that when one is produced the other is also produced
5 they are the same substantial entity (*dravya, rdzas*), in that the production, abiding, and cessation of the two occur simultaneously

Main minds are, for example, the five sense perceivers and the mental perceivers. Mental factors are commonly described in a list of fifty-one which are divided into six categories, although this list is not all-inclusive. The six categories are:

1 omnipresent (*sarvatraga, kun 'gro*)
2 determining (**viṣhayapratiniyama, yul nges*)
3 virtuous (*kushala, dge ba*)
4 root afflictions (*mūlaklesha, rtsa nyon*)
5 secondary afflictions (*upaklesha, nye nyon*)
6 changeable (*anyathābhāva, gzhan 'gyur*)

So-called because they accompany every main mind, the five omnipresent factors are:

1 feeling (*vedanā, tshor ba*) – that factor which experiences an object as pleasurable, painful, or neutral
2 discrimination (*samjñā, 'du shes*) which apprehends the uncommon signs of the object
3 intention (*chetanā, sems pa*) which directs the mind to the object
4 mental engagement (*manasi-kāra, yid la byed pa*) which directs the mind to the particular object of observation
5 contact (*sparsha, reg pa*) which serves as the basis for the generation of the feelings of pleasure, pain, or neutrality

The five determining factors are:

1 aspiration (*chhanda, 'dun pa*)
2 belief (*adhimokṣha, mos pa*)

3 mindfulness (*smṛti, dran pa*)
4 stabilization (*samādhi, ting nge 'dzin*)
5 wisdom (*prajñā, shes rab*)

If one of these is present all five are present; however these do not accompany all minds; they accompany all virtuous minds and no others.

The remaining groups of mental factors do not function as a simultaneous unit in the way that the first two do. There are eleven virtuous mental factors:

1 faith (*shraddhā, dad pa*)
2 shame (*hrī, ngo tsha shes pa*)
3 embarrassment (*apatrāpya, khrel yod pa*)
4 non-attachment (*alobha, ma chags pa*)
5 non-hatred (*adveṣha, zhe sdang med pa*)
6 non-ignorance (*amoha, gti mug med pa*)
7 effort (*vīrya, brtson 'grus*)
8 pliancy (*prasrabdhi, shin tu sbyangs pa*)
9 conscientiousness (*apramāda, bag yod pa*)
10 equanimity (*upekṣhā, btang snyoms*)
11 non-harmfulness (*avihiṃsā, rnam par mi 'tshe ba*)

These can never occur at the same time as any of the afflictions – root or secondary. Although it is possible for all eleven to occur simultaneously, it is not the case that they always do; this Sautrāntika assertion differs from the system of Vasubandhu's *Treasury of Knowledge* (*Adhidharmakosha*) which states that if one is present all are necessarily so.

There are six root afflictions:

1 desire (*rāga, 'dod chags*)
2 anger (*pratigha, khong khro*)
3 pride (*māna, nga rgyal*)
4 ignorance (*avidyā, ma rig pa*)
5 doubt (*vichikitsā, the tshom*)
6 afflicted view (*dṛṣhṭi, lta ba nyon mongs can*)

as well as twenty secondary afflictions:

1 belligerence (*krodha, khro ba*)
2 resentment (*upanāha, 'khon 'dzin*)
3 concealment (*mrakṣha, 'chab pa*)
4 spite (*pradāsa, 'tshig pa*)
5 jealousy (*īrṣhyā, phrag dog*)
6 miserliness (*mātsarya, ser sna*
7 deceit (*māyā, sgyu*)
8 dissimulation (*shāṭhya, g.yo*)
9 haughtiness (*mada, rgyags pa*)
10 harmfulness (*vihiṃsā, rnam pa 'tshe ba*)
11 non-shame (*āhrīkya, ngo tsha med pa*)
12 non-embarrassment (*anapatrāpya, khrel med pa*)
13 lethargy (*styāna, rmugs pa*)
14 excitement (*auddhatya, rgod pa*)
15 non-faith (*āshraddhya, ma dad pa*)
16 laziness (*kausīdya, le lo*)
17 non-conscientiousness (*pramāda, bag med pa*)
18 forgetfulness (*muṣhitasmṛtitā, brjed nges pa*)
19 non-introspection (*asaṃprajanya, shes bzhin ma yin pa*)
20 distraction (*vikṣhepa, rnam par g.yeng ba*)

It is not possible for all the root afflictions to be present simultaneously; for example, if desire is present, hatred will not be, and vice versa; similarly for the secondary afflictions, those of the type of desire, such as jealousy, will not be present at the same time as those of the type of hatred, such as belligerence or resentment. However, secondary afflictions and root afflictions of the same type such as hatred and belligerence can be present simultaneously although they do not have to be.

The four changeable factors are:

1 sleep (*middha, gnyid*)
2 contrition (*kaukritya, 'gyod pa*)
3 investigation (*vitarka, rtog pa*)
4 analysis (*vichāra, dpyod pa*)

They are changeable in the sense that they can become either virtuous or non-virtuous depending on the motivation which impels them.

Through study of 'Awareness and Knowledge' one comes to know what the different types of minds are, and moreover, which sorts of minds it is helpful to develop and which should be abandoned. One can understand what the state of one's mind is at present as well as into what it can eventually be transformed. With this as a basis, it is then far more meaningful both to engage in further study of the stages involved in the process of transformation and actually to enter into it.

PART TWO

Translation

Lati Rinbochay's commentary has been interwoven with Ge-shay Jam-bel-sam-pel's *Presentation of Awareness and Knowledge*, with the latter indented to set it off from Lati Rinbochay's explanation.

1. *Consciousness*

The title of Ge-shay Jam-bel-sam-pel's text is:

> *Presentation of Awareness and Knowledge*
> *Composite of All the Important Points*
> *Opener of the Eye of New Intelligence*

Small children are at first unable to distinguish good and bad, what will help or harm. Then becoming able to think, they come to understand these roughly. Such an understanding is called awareness or knowing. They then learn to distinguish more and more subtly what will help or harm, what should be undertaken and what avoided, and this too is awareness. Thus, it is necessary to understand well the presentation of awareness and knowledge; it is an explanation of what accords and does not accord with the fact, what is and is not valid.

In general, a great many topics are set forth in such a presentation, but here we are dealing with the important ones; this explanation is a composite of all the important points. It is called opener of the eye of new intelligence because it causes us to open the eye of wisdom in our own continuum, to attain the wisdom that understands well, the awareness that correctly distinguishes good and bad. If one has good eyes, one can understand where it is and is not suitable to go; similarly, wisdom or awareness is able to distinguish good and bad. It is called *new* intelligence because in the past we have not identified it well.

Ge-shay Jam-bel-sam-pel's text begins with an expression of worship:

> Having bowed down to the glorious Lo-sang-drak-ba (bLo-bzang-grags-pa)
> Emanation of Mañjughoṣha, treasury of wisdom, I extend this presentation of awareness and knowledge, composite of all the important points,
> In order to increase the clarity of knowledge of those with low intelligence.

Mañjughoṣha appeared in the form of Lo-sang-drak-ba, or Tsong-ka-pa, in order that the teaching might benefit many people; he spread widely Buddha Shākyamuni's teaching and rectified it. Therefore, the author begins his text with an obeisance to Tsong-ka-pa.

Buddhas and Bodhisattvas have perfect wisdom. Mañjughoṣha, appearing in the form of a deity, embodies the composite of the wisdom of all the Buddhas and thus is called a treasury of wisdom. Moreover, Mañjughoṣha can, when pleased, bestow perfect wisdom on others with a mere glance of his eye and for this reason also he is a treasury of wisdom.

He is called *mañju* – gentle, agreeable, soft – because he is free from the harshness of afflictive and non-afflictive obstructions. He is called *ghoṣha* – speech, sound, melody – because he is the lord of speech and because his speech possesses the sixty qualities of vocalization. He is called *shrī* [Mañjushrī] – glorious – because he has the glory of the completion of the two collections, merit and wisdom. He appeared in the form of a human, as Lo-sang-drak-ba, by the power of great compassion and aspirational prayers – that is, by his own power, not by that of contaminated actions and afflictions as in ordinary birth.

Here the author is making the three types of homage, through body, speech, and mind. Physical homage means to raise with a pure mind even one finger or bow the head in respect; a verbal homage is any praise spoken with a pure mind; mental homage is a pure mind of respect itself. The author, having paid homage with body, speech, and mind, says that he will compose this presentation of awareness and knowledge which is a composite of all the important points.

This presentation of awareness and knowledge has three parts: definitions, divisions, and the meaning of each division.

Definitions

The definition of an awareness is a knower. The definition of a consciousness is that which is clear and knowing. [1b.2–3]

All four schools of tenets, Vaibhāṣhika, Sautrāntika, Chittamātra, and Mādhyamika, use these same definitions. However, there are those who, based on Dharmakīrti's *Commentary on (Dignāga's) 'Compendium on Prime Cognition'* and Shāntirakṣhita's *Ornament for the Middle Way* (*Madhyamakālaṃkāra*), posit as the definition of a consciousness 'non-matter which is clear'. This definition is incorrect because non-matter which is clear is a negative (*pratiṣhedha, dgag pa*), whereas consciousness is a positive phenomenon (*vidhi, sgrub pa*). Thus, when 'non-matter which is clear' appears to the mind, an aspect which is a negative has to appear, but when consciousness appears to the mind, a positive aspect has to appear. This would entail the fault that an awareness which knows how to associate the name – 'consciousness' – and the meaning – 'non-matter which is clear' – would be realizing both a positive and a negative phenomenon and would mean that positive and negative phenomena are not mutually exclusive [which in fact they are].

In some presentations of awareness and knowledge another objection is raised against those who posit non-matter which is clear as the definition of consciousness. The objectors say that whatever is non-matter which is clear is not necessarily a consciousness as is the case, for example, with emptiness. Their referent for saying that emptiness (*shūnyatā, stong pa nyid*) is clear is a passage in the root text of Dharmakīrti's *Commentary on (Dignāga's) 'Compendium on Prime Cognition'* which says that the nature of the mind is clear light (*ābhāsvarā*, *'od gsal*) with the word 'clear' meaning, in that context, emptiness. However, this point is not convincing since the 'clear' of 'non-matter which is clear' and of 'clear light' are not the same. The term 'clear' in the former refers to the object's appearing to or illuminating the mind;[29] that of the latter refers to the mind as having a nature without defilement.

Another specious objection that is raised to 'non-matter which is clear' as the definition of consciousness is that, according to the Mahāyāna, a Buddha's physical body and sense powers are not matter and are clear and thus would have to be consciousnesses. However, the reason for saying that a Buddha's body and sense powers are clear is that their nature is without defilement, without the obstructiveness of flesh, bones, and so forth, and in that sense have a nature of clear light. As before, this meaning of 'clear' and its meaning in the definition of consciousness are quite different and thus the objection is not convincing.

Although neither of the latter two objections is considered to refute this as the definition of consciousness, the first – that of the mixing of positive and negative phenomena – does, and thus, in our system [that of Pan-chen Sö-nam-drak-ba] it is incorrect to posit non-matter which is clear as the definition of a consciousness. Instead, the correct definition is: 'that which is clear and knowing'.]

Nevertheless, there are varying interpretations of its meaning.[30] Some say that 'clear' refers to the object's appearing clearly from its own side to the appearance factor of the mind and 'knowing' refers to the subject, the awareness, apprehending or knowing the object. There are others who say that 'clear' and 'knowing' both refer to the subject's perceiving the object and thus the definition means 'that which illuminates and knows'.

It is not sufficient to posit as the definition of a consciousness merely 'that which is clear', for there are many things which are clear without being consciousnesses such as the sense powers, glass, the moon, and the sun. All schools of tenets identify the sense powers as clear form (*rūpa-prasāda, gzugs dang ba*) to which the object appears, and the Vaibhāṣhikas say further that the sense powers *see* their objects; however, something cannot be a consciousness merely due to the object's appearing to it; there must also be a knowing of that object, and thus the definition of consciousness is specified as that which is clear and knowing, thereby eliminating the sense powers.

According to the Sautrāntika system, whatever is known by a consciousness does not necessarily have to appear to it as in the case of implicit realization and thus one could not posit as the definition of a consciousness: 'that to which an object appears' (*yul snang ba*)[31] or: 'that to which an object reflects' (*yul 'char ba*).

For example, the exalted wisdom of meditative equipoise (*samāhita-jñāna, mnyam bzhag ye shes*) which is in one-pointed concentration on the selflessness of the person (*pudgala-nairātmya, gang zag gi bdag med*) knows (*rig*) the selflessness of the person, but that selflessness does not appear (*snang*) to it. This is because the selflessness of the person is permanent and only an appearing object of a thought consciousness whereas the wisdom of meditative equipoise which is in one-pointed concentration on the selflessness of the person is a direct perceiver. In Sautrāntika, appearing object of direct perception and impermanent thing are synonymous and appearing object of thought and permanent phenomenon are synonymous, and thus a permanent phenomenon such as the selflessness of the person cannot *appear* to a direct perceiver such as the wisdom of meditative equipoise although it can be *known* by it. That wisdom explicitly (*vastutaḥ, dngos su*) knows the aggregates which are devoid of a self of persons and through the force of that knowledge implicitly (*sāmarthyāt, shugs kyis*) knows the selflessness of the person.

The three – awareness, knower, and consciousness – are synonymous.

Divisions

There are three divisions of awareness and knowledge: into seven, three, and two. The division into seven consists of direct perception, inference, subsequent cognition, correct assumption, appearance without ascertainment, doubt, and wrong consciousness. [1b.3–2a.2]

2. *Direct Perceivers*

> *Direct Perceivers*
> The explanation of direct perceivers has two parts: definitions and divisions. The definition of a direct perceiver is a non-mistaken knower that is free from conceptuality. [2a.2–3]

It would be sufficient to posit 'non-mistaken consciousness' as the definition of direct perceiver; 'free from conceptuality' is included in order to eliminate the Vaisheṣhikas' mistaken view that the sense consciousnesses are conceptual.

There are many interpretations of 'free from conceptuality'. Some say that it means 'not conceptual'. This, however, is too broad, for a person is not conceptual, that is, is not a conceptual consciousness. Nonetheless, a person is not free from conceptuality because of engaging in conceptual apprehension of objects.

Another possible meaning of 'free from conceptuality' is 'free from the substantial entity of conceptuality'. However, whatever is free from conceptuality is not necessarily free from the substantial entity of conceptuality. For instance, a self-knowing direct perceiver experiencing a conceptual consciousness is itself free from conceptuality since it is a direct perceiver, but it is not free from the substantial entity of conceptuality because it is the same substantial entity as the conceptual mind it is experiencing. A self-knowing direct perceiver is always the same substantial entity as the mind it experiences.

Another meaning posited for 'free from conceptuality' is 'free from the self-reverse of conceptuality'. This also is incorrect, for particular instances of conceptuality, although free from the self-reverse of conceptuality since the self-reverse of conceptuality is only conceptuality in general, are not free from conceptuality.

What can be posited correctly as the definition of 'free from conceptuality'? In our own system it is: that which is free from being a determinative knower that apprehends a sound [generality] (*shabda-sāmānya, sgra spyi*) and a meaning [generality] (*artha-sāmānya, don spyi*) as suitable to be mixed'.

Thus, a non-conceptual consciousness is defined as being that which lacks the attributes defining a conceptual consciousness – that is, lacks being a determinative knower that apprehends sound and meaning generalities as suitable to be mixed.

All thought consciousnesses are determinative knowers (**adhyavasāya-saṃvedana, zhen rig*) and all direct perceivers are non-determinative. The meaning of 'determinative' is that such a consciousness thinks, 'This is such and such,' 'That is such and such.'[32]

The sound and meaning generalities which a determinative knower apprehends as suitable to be mixed can be explained in two ways. With respect to the first, if someone describes an object that you have never seen, such as an ocean, the image that appears to your mind based on the description is a sound generality. When you see an ocean for the first time, without having been told beforehand what it is, the image appearing to your mind is just a meaning generality. When someone tells you, 'This is an ocean', the sound and meaning generalities then appear to your mind as if associated – that is to say mixed.

With respect to the second explanation, if someone says the word 'ocean' to you without your knowing its meaning, the image generated at that time is a sound generality, a mere reverberation of the sound 'ocean'. When someone says the word 'ocean' and you know its meaning, the image that appears to your mind is a meaning generality. Although not the actual object, the image appears to be that object.

The reason that the definition specifies that sound and meaning generalities are apprehended as *suitable* to be mixed is that it is possible to have a thought consciousness apprehending only a sound generality, one apprehending only a meaning generality, or one apprehending the two as if mixed.

The definition of direct perceiver specifies that as well as being free from conceptuality it must be a non-mistaken knower. Such a knower is non-mistaken with regard to its appearing object. It would be incorrect to posit as the meaning of non-mistaken knower 'that which is non-mistaken with regard to its object of engagement'. For an inferential cognizer is non-mistaken with regard to its object of engagement but is nonetheless not a direct perceiver because it is mistaken with regard to its appearing object. It is mistaken in the sense that its appearing object is a meaning generality, a mental image of its object of engagement, which appears to it to be the actual object, like a mirror image appearing to be a face.

Also, since object of comprehension (*vineya, gzhal bya*) and object of engagement are synonyms, it would be equally incorrect to posit as the meaning of non-mistaken 'non-mistaken with regard to its object of comprehension'. An inferential cognizer, though mistaken, is non-mistaken with regard to its object of comprehension.

It would also be incorrect to posit 'not affected by any of the four superficial causes of error'. This again is too limited, for although any consciousness affected by one of the four causes of error is mistaken, any mistaken consciousness is not necessarily polluted by one of these. For example, a thought consciousness realizing impermanence is mistaken with regard to its appearing object in the sense that a meaning generality of impermanence appears to be impermanence itself, but is not affected by any of the four adventitious causes of error. These four are:

1 the cause of error existing in the object (*viṣhaya, yul*)
2 the cause of error existing in the basis (*āshraya, rten*)
3 the cause of error existing in the abode (*sthāna, gnas*)
4 the cause of error existing in the immediately preceding condition (*samanantara-pratyaya, de ma thag rkyen*)

An example of a cause of error existing in the object is a consciousness perceiving a circle of fire due to a firebrand being twirled around quickly. An example of a cause of error existing in the basis is an eye consciousness which sees a single moon as double due to a fault in the eye. An example of a cause of error existing in the abode or place is an eye consciousness which sees trees as moving when one is riding in a boat or car. An example of a cause of error existing in the immediately preceding condition is an eye consciousness which sees everything as red when one is overcome by anger.

> The definition of a direct prime cognizer [that is, a directly perceiving prime cognizer] is a new incontrovertible non-mistaken knower that is free from conceptuality. [2b.1]

The meanings of 'free from conceptuality' and 'non-mistaken' are the same as in the definition of direct perceiver. 'New' means that the object of the consciousness is being met with, or comprehended, for the first time. 'Incontrovertible' means that this cognizer has eliminated superimpositions with regard to its object – it has obtained or got at its object of distinguishment (*bcad don thob pa*). This means that it realizes its object.

> When direct perceivers are divided, there are four: sense, mental, self-knowing, and yogic direct perceivers. [2b.1]

When direct prime cognizers are divided, there are also four: sense, mental, self-knowing, and yogic direct prime cognizers.

> *Sense direct perceivers.* The definition of a sense direct perceiver is a non-mistaken non-conceptual knower that is produced from its own uncommon empowering condition, a physical sense power. [2b.2]

The uncommon empowering condition of, for example, a sense direct perceiver apprehending a form is the eye sense power; that of a sense direct perceiver apprehending a sound is the ear sense power; of a sense direct perceiver apprehending an odour, the nose sense power; of a sense direct perceiver apprehending a taste, the tongue sense power; and of a sense direct perceiver apprehending a tangible object, the body sense power.

> When sense direct perceivers are divided, there are five: those apprehending forms, sounds, odours, tastes, and tangible objects. The definition of a sense direct perceiver apprehending a form (**rūpa-grahaṇa-indriya-pratyakṣha, gzugs 'dzin dbang mngon*) is a non-mistaken non-conceptual knower that is produced in dependence on its own uncommon empowering condition, the eye sense power, and an observed object condition, a form. Apply this [definition] similarly to the other [divisions of sense direct perceivers]. [2b.2–4]

It is also possible to omit the phrase 'and an observed object condition, a form'. Either way is correct.

The definition of a sense direct perceiver apprehending a sound is a non-mistaken non-conceptual knower that is produced in dependence on its own uncommon empowering condition, the ear sense power, and an observed object condition, a sound. The definition of a sense direct perceiver apprehending an odour is a non-mistaken non-conceptual knower that is produced in dependence on its own uncommon empowering condition, the nose sense power, and an observed object condition, an odour. The definition of a sense direct perceiver apprehending a taste is a non-mistaken non-conceptual knower that is produced in dependence on its own uncommon empowering condition, the tongue sense power, and an observed object condition, a taste. The definition of a sense direct perceiver apprehending a tangible object is a non-mistaken non-conceptual knower that is produced in dependence on its own uncommon empowering condition, the body sense power, and an observed object condition, a tangible object.

> *Mental direct perceivers.* The definition of a mental direct perceiver is a non-mistaken non-conceptual knower that arises from its own uncommon empowering condition, a mental sense power. [2b.4–3a.1]

The mental sense power (*mana-indriya, yid dbang*) is whichever of the six consciousnesses has immediately preceded it.

> When mental direct perceivers are divided, there are two: those that are and are not 'indicated on this occasion'. [3a.1]

Sūtra says, 'Consciousnesses of forms are of two types, those depending on the eye and those depending on the mind.' 'Those depending on the eye' refers to sense consciousnesses, that is, consciousnesses whose uncommon empowering condition is a physical sense power, in this case the eye; 'those depending on the mind' refers to mental consciousnesses, that is, to mental direct perceivers whose uncommon empowering condition is a mental sense power, in this case a former moment of sense direct perception which induces it. The basis for the division of mental direct perceivers into those that are and are not 'indicated on this occasion' is the portion of the sūtra statement, 'those depending on the mind', and thus, mental direct perceivers indicated on this occasion are those induced by sense direct perceivers apprehending any of the five sense objects – forms, sounds, odours, tastes, or tangible objects.

Examples of mental direct perceivers that are not indicated on this occasion are mental direct perceivers induced by states arisen from meditation (*bhāvanā-mayī, sgom byung*) such as the five clairvoyances. These five, which can be generated in the continuum of an ordinary being, are:

1 the clairvoyance of magical emanation (*ṛddhi-abhijñā, rdsu 'phrul gyi mngon shes*)
2 the clairvoyance of divine eye (*divya-chakṣhur-abhijñā, lha'i mig gi mngon shes*)

3 the clairvoyance of divine ear (*divya-shrotra-abhijñā, lha'i rna ba'i mngon shes*)
4 the clairvoyance of memory of former lifetimes (*pūrva-nivāsānusmṛti-abhijñā, sngon gyi gnas rjes su dran pa'i mngon shes*)
5 the clairvoyance of knowing others' minds (*para-chitta-jñāna-abhijñā, gzhan sems shes pa'i mngon shes*)

The power of magical emanation is the ability to display various emanations and to increase or decrease their number. That of the divine eye is the ability to see the coarse and subtle forms of the one billion worlds of this world system. Coarse forms are ordinary forms whereas subtle forms are beyond the capacities of an ordinary eye or ear but are perceivable by those with such clairvoyance. The clairvoyance of divine ear is the ability to hear the coarse and subtle sounds of this world system. The clairvoyance of memory of former lifetimes is the ability to remember one's own and others' former lifetimes.

These five are induced by states arisen from meditation, and thus the clairvoyances of divine eye and ear should not be understood as eye or ear consciousnesses. They are mental consciousnesses even though the names eye and ear are imputed to them.

Other mental direct perceivers not indicated on this occasion – that is, not induced by sense direct perceivers – and also not induced by states arisen from meditation are self-knowers and also the karmic clairvoyance of a being in the intermediate state [after death and before taking rebirth]. The latter is a clairvoyance that one has due to the power of previous actions (*karma, las*) from merely being born in the intermediate state (*bar do*) and is a contaminated clairvoyance enabling one to know coarse objects but not subtle qualities.

> The definition of a mental direct perceiver indicated on this occasion is a non-conceptual non-mistaken other-knower indicated on this occasion that arises from its own uncommon empowering condition, a mental sense power. [3a.1–2]

It is called an other-knower because it is not a consciousness that is turned inwards, is not a self-knower, but is a consciousness that engages external objects.

> When mental direct perceivers indicated on this occasion are divided, there are five, ranging from those apprehending forms to those apprehending tangible objects. [3a.2]

Mental direct perceivers indicated on this occasion take as their objects only the five sense objects. Those mental direct perceivers which take phenomena – here meaning those things that are only objects of the mental consciousness such as subtle impermanence – as their objects are yogic direct perceivers and as such are mental direct perceivers, but are not those indicated on this occasion.

> With respect to how mental direct perceivers indicated on this occasion are produced, there are three assertions: alternating production, production of three types, and production only at the end of a continuum. From among these the mode of alternating production is as follows: the first moment of a sense direct perceiver apprehending a form is produced; subsequently the first moment of a mental direct perceiver apprehending the form is produced; subsequently the second moment of the sense direct perceiver apprehending the form is produced, and so on. They assert that between each moment of sense direct perception a moment of mental direct perception is produced.
>
> The mode of production of three types is asserted as follows: the three – the second moment of a sense direct perceiver apprehending a form, the first moment of a mental direct perceiver apprehending that form, and the self-knowing direct perceiver experiencing those two – are produced simultaneously. In brief, it is asserted that two types directed outward and one type directed inward are produced at one time.
>
> The mode of production only at the end of a continuum is the thought of the foremost father [Tsong-ka-pa] and his spiritual son [Gyel-tsap]. Here a mental direct perceiver apprehending a form is produced only at the end of the last moment of a sense direct perceiver apprehending a form. Furthermore, it is clear in the textbook [Pan-chen Sö-nam-drak-ba's commentary on Dharmakīrti's *Commentary on (Dignāga's) 'Compendium on Prime*

Cognition'] that it is necessary to assert that in the continuum of one who looks nearby [i.e., an ordinary being] no more than one smallest moment of a mental direct perceiver apprehending a form is produced.

'Indicated on this occasion' must be understood as referring to the occasion where it is said [in sūtra]: 'Consciousnesses of forms are of two types: those depending on the eye and on the mind (*manas, yid*).'

Mental direct perceivers not indicated on this occasion are such [consciousnesses] as a clairvoyance which knows another's mind. [3a.2–3b.4]

Sa-gya Pandita in his *Treasury of Reasoning* identifies these differing explanations of the mode of production of these mental direct perceivers as having been set forth by three Indian scholars [all commentators on Dharmakīrti's *Commentary on (Dignāga's) 'Compendium on Prime Cognition'*]. Alternating production was set forth by Prajñākaragupta, production in three types by the brahmin Shaṅkarānanda, and production only at the end of a continuum by the master Dharmottara. Sa-gya Pandita himself refutes alternating production as well as production only at the end of a continuum and propounds the second, production in three types. However, in our own system, we reject the first and second and explain that the mental direct perceivers indicated in the above quote are produced only at the end of a continuum.

Alternating production is not feasible because if, between the first and second moments of sense direct perception, a moment of mental direct perception were produced, there would not be an unbroken continuum of sense direct perception, and the first moment of sense direct perception could not be the direct cause of its next moment [whereas it must be].

Production in three types is incorrect both in terms of its verbal designation and meaning. The fallacy of the verbal designation is that although three types are mentioned, there are in fact either four or two. The four are comprised of two types directed outwards – the second moment of a sense direct perceiver apprehending a form and the first moment of a mental direct perceiver apprehending the form – and two directed inwards – a self-knower experiencing each of the two directed outwards. The proponents of production in three types, however, do not posit two self-knowers since they are the same in being faced inwards, but to this our own system responds that, in that case, the second moment of the sense direct perceiver apprehending the form and the first moment of the mental direct perceiver apprehending the form should also not be posited separately since they are the same in being directed outwards. It is in this sense that one might say that there is production in two types, one directed outwards and one inwards. In any case, it is not suitable to call this production in three types.

The meaning of production in three types is also incorrect because Buddha said that each sentient being has only one continuum of each consciousness. Thus it is incorrect to posit the production of many consciousnesses, that is, to assert the simultaneous production of one moment of a sense direct perceiver apprehending a form, one moment of a mental direct perceiver apprehending that form, and self-knowers experiencing those two. It is true that all six consciousnesses can be produced simultaneously, but they all have different objects, whereas these that the proponents of production in three types are asserting as produced simultaneously all observe the same object.

Kay-drup Rin-bo-chay, in his *Clearing Away Darkness of Mind with Respect to the Seven Treatises*, essentially asserts this second mode of production although he does not call it production in three types. He says that this does not contradict Buddha's statement that each sentient being has only one continuum of consciousness if one interprets it as meaning similarity of reverse type (*ldog pa rigs gcig*) and not similarity of substantial type (*rdzas rigs gcig*). According to him, there is no fault in the production at one time of many consciousnesses of one substantial type although there would be a fault in the production of many consciousnesses of one reverse type. Thus, there is no fault in the simultaneous production of a direct perceiver apprehending a form and the self-knower experiencing it – consciousnesses which are one substantial entity – but there would be a fault in the simultaneous production of two moments of a mental direct perceiver apprehending a form – consciousnesses that are one reverse type [that is, exactly the same general type].

The third assertion, production only at the end of a continuum, accords with our own system and is the thought of Tsong-ka-pa and his spiritual son [Gyel-tsap]. We can take as an example the production of five moments of a sense direct perceiver apprehending a form. These are five consecutive moments paying attention to one object, and only at the end of the continuum of those five moments is one moment of a mental direct perceiver apprehending the form produced. Our text, as well as Pan-chen Sö-nam-drak-ba's textbook (on which this text is based), Jam-yang-shay-ba's textbook, and all the others agree in asserting production only at the end of a continuum as the correct explanation of how mental direct perceivers indicated on this occasion are produced.

Pan-chen Sö-nam-drak-ba and Jam-yang-shay-ba also accord in asserting that not more than one smallest moment of a mental direct perceiver indicated on this occasion is generated. Thus, in the continuums of ordinary beings such as ourselves these are cases of knowers to which an object appears but is not ascertained and are very hidden phenomena (*atyantaparokṣha, shin tu lkog gyur*).

This is true only of mental direct perceivers indicated on this occasion. Those not so indicated, such as clairvoyances and self-knowers in the continuums of ordinary beings are able to ascertain, that is, to realize, their objects.

> *Self-knowing direct perceivers.* The definition of a self-knower is that which has the aspect of an apprehender. [3b.4]

There are two types of consciousnesses: other-knowers and self-knowers. That which engages an object other than an internal consciousness is an other-knower; it is a consciousness directed outwards (*kha phyi lta gi shes pa*). That which experiences an internal consciousness is a self-knower; because it engages an internal consciousness, it is said to be directed inwards (*kha nang lta gi shes pa*). Applying this to the illustration of an eye consciousness apprehending blue, the eye consciousness itself is an other-knower and the consciousness which experiences that eye consciousness is a self-knower.

We need to identify the apprehended (*grāhya, bzung ba* and the apprehender (*grāhaka, 'dzin pa*). The blue which is the object of the eye consciousness apprehending blue is the apprehended, whereas the eye consciousness itself is the apprehender. Furthermore, the eye consciousness apprehending blue sees the aspect of blue and is thus called that which has the aspect of the apprehended (*grāhya-ākāra, bzung rnam*). The consciousness which experiences that eye consciousness sees the apprehender itself and is thus called that which has the aspect of an apprehender (*grāhaka-ākāra, 'dzin rnam*).

> The definition of a self-knowing direct perceiver is that which is non-conceptual non-mistaken and has the aspect of an apprehender. [3b.4]

Thus, we have had the definitions of a self-knower and a self-knowing direct perceiver; if we add to this the element of being a prime cognizer, then the definition of a self-knowing direct prime cognizer is: 'that which is new incontrovertible non-conceptual non-mistaken and has the aspect of an apprehender'.

> When self-knowing direct perceivers are divided, there are three: those that are prime cognizers, those that are subsequent cognizers, and those to which an object appears but is not ascertained. [4a.1]

A self-knower experiencing a wrong consciousness is the same entity as that consciousness, but it is not a wrong consciousness itself; thus, it is still one of the three – a prime cognizer, subsequent cognizer, or an awareness to which an object appears but is not ascertained.

There are four possibilities between prime cognizer and

self-knower, between subsequent cognizer and self-knower, and between awareness to which an object appears but is not ascertained and self-knower.[33] The first moment of a self-knower experiencing an eye consciousness apprehending blue is both a self-knower and a prime cognizer. The second moment of the self-knower experiencing that eye consciousness is a self-knower but not a prime cognizer. The first moment of an eye consciousness apprehending blue is a prime cognizer but not a self-knower, and the second moment of an eye consciousness apprehending blue is neither a prime cognizer nor a self-knower.

The four possibilities between subsequent cognizer and self-knower are much the same. The second moment of a self-knower experiencing an eye consciousness apprehending blue is both a subsequent cognizer and a self-knower. The first moment of a self-knower experiencing an eye consciousness apprehending blue is a self-knower but not a subsequent cognizer. The second moment of an eye consciousness apprehending blue is a subsequent cognizer but not a self-knower. Something which is neither is the first moment of an eye consciousness apprehending blue.

Similarly, there are four possibilities between an awareness to which an object appears but is not ascertained and a self-knower. The self-knower in the continuum of an ordinary being which experiences a mental direct perceiver apprehending a form is both an awareness to which an object appears but is not ascertained and a self-knower. The self-knower experiencing an eye consciousness apprehending a form is a self-knower but is not a mind to which an object appears but is not ascertained. A mental direct perceiver in the continuum of an ordinary being which apprehends a form is an awareness to which an object appears but is not ascertained but is not a self-knower. An eye consciousness apprehending a form is neither of these two.

Yogic direct perceivers. The definition of a yogic direct perceiver is a non-conceptual non-mistaken exalted knower in the continuum of a Superior that is produced from a meditative stabilization which is a union of calm abiding and special insight and which has become its own uncommon empowering condition. [4a.1–2]

Pur-bu-jok posits this definition a little differently. He defines a yogic direct perceiver as: 'A non-conceptual non-mistaken other-knower in the continuum of a Superior that is produced from a meditative stabilization which is a union of calm abiding and special insight and which has become its own uncommon empowering condition'.

Thus, he substitutes 'other-knower' for 'exalted knower'. The reason for so specifying 'other-knower' is that there is a problem with regard to a self-knowing direct perceiver experiencing a yogic direct perceiver. Let us discuss this.

A self-knowing direct perceiver experiencing a yogic direct perceiver and that yogic direct perceiver are established in dependence on one causal collection (*dngos rgyu tshogs pa gcig*). They are thus one substantial entity in establishment and abiding and have the same causes in that whatever is a cause of the one is a cause of the other and vice versa. Since a yogic direct perceiver is produced from a meditative stabilization which is a union of calm abiding and special insight and which has become its own uncommon empowering condition, a self-knower experiencing that yogic direct perceiver must also be produced from the same meditative stabilization. Such a self-knower would then fulfill the definition of a yogic direct perceiver, and thus, yogic direct perceivers would include some self-knowers. [Since this is absurd] the term 'other-knower' is added to the definition in order specifically to eliminate self-knowers.

However, the thought of our text, as well as of Jam-yang-shay-ba and others, is that such a specific elimination is not necessary. For, a yogic direct perceiver and the self-knower experiencing it do have the same causes, but this does not necessarily mean that they have the same uncommon empowering condition. A self-knower experiencing a yogic direct perceiver does not arise by the power of meditation – does not arise from the force of a meditative stabilization which is a union of calm abiding and special insight – but arises ancillarily (*shar la*). It merely comes along with the yogic direct perceiver and thus cannot be said to have the same uncommon empowering condition.

Similarly, a sense direct perceiver apprehending a form and the self-knower experiencing it have the same group of causes but have different uncommon empowering conditions. The uncommon empowering condition of the sense direct perceiver is a physical sense power – the eye sense power. The uncommon empowering condition of the self-knower experiencing it is a mental sense power.

Since those things which have the same causes do not necessarily have the same uncommon empowering condition, one would not posit the meditative stabilization which is a union of calm abiding and special insight as the uncommon empowering condition of a self-knower experiencing a yogic direct perceiver. Thus, there is no need to specify 'other-knower' in the definition of a yogic direct perceiver in order to eliminate self-knowers, and Ge-shay Jam-bel-sam-pel's definition is correct as stated.

> When yogic direct perceivers are divided there are three: those of Hearers (*Shrāvaka, Nyan thos*), Solitary Realizers (*Pratyeka-buddha, Rang rgyal*), and Mahāyānists. [4a.2]

This division is made from the viewpoint of the basis [the person who possesses it]. If yogic direct perceivers are divided from the viewpoint of their entities, there are those of the paths of seeing, meditation, and no more learning. If they are divided from the viewpoint of their aspects, one can posit sixteen, having the aspects of the sixteen attributes of the four noble truths, impermanence and so forth.[34] One can also posit yogic direct perceivers having the aspects of coarse and subtle selflessness.

How does one establish that a yogic direct perceiver exists? If the wisdom cognizing selflessness is cultivated without separating from the conditions of meditation, one can attain very clear perception of the object of meditation [that is, one can come to realize it directly, without relying on an image] because its basis is stable and it is a mental phenomenon that does not require renewed exertion with respect to that to which it has already become conditioned. Its basis is stable because the mind cognizing selflessness has as its basis clear light. It does not require or depend on renewed exertion because once one has become conditioned to it, it arises automatically; it is unlike, for instance, high-jumping where, no matter how much you practise, each time you jump you must again make effort.

This reasoning establishing yogic direct perceivers is necessary, for otherwise one could not establish the existence of omniscience and so forth. If, when cultivating the wisdom realizing selflessness, one does not become separate from the conditions for cultivating it and becomes thoroughly conditioned to it, it is possible to extend it endlessly. Its increase is immeasurable, whereas for other activities like high-jumping there is a measure, a limit, to how skilled one can become. The difference is that one does not have to depend on renewed effort for those things to which the mind has become familiarized.

There is also a reasoning establishing the existence of self-knowers. One can state the syllogism, 'The subject, an eye consciousness apprehending blue, is a consciousness possessing an experiencer of itself because it is a consciousness of which there is memory after its own time.' This proof is used by all those tenet systems which assert self-knowers – Sautrāntika, Chittamātra, and Yogāchāra-Svātantrika. Vaibhāṣhika, Sautrāntika-Svātantrika, and Prāsaṅgika do not assert self-knowers. There is no clear source on whether or not the Sautrāntikas following scripture, that is, those following Vasubandhu's *Treasury of Knowledge* (*Abhidharmakosha*), assert self-knowers or not. Based on the fact that the root assertions of Sautrāntikas in general are that they assert external objects and self-knowers, many texts say that the Sautrāntikas following scripture do assert self-knowers. Jam-yang-shay-ba said that they do not, but his next incarnation, Gön-chok-jik-may-wang-bo (dKon-mchog-'jigs-med-dbang-po, 1728–91), said that they do.

> It is said that self-knowing and yogic direct perceivers must be mental direct perceivers.[35] [4a.2]

That self-knowing direct perceivers are mental ones means that, for example, a self-knower experiencing an eye consciousness apprehending blue does not depend on the eye sense power as its uncommon empowering condition, but depends on a mental sense power. Therefore, a self-knower is a mental and not a sense direct perceiver.

Saying that a yogic direct perceiver must be a mental one is important in terms of a discussion of a Buddha, for this eliminates that self-knowing and sense direct perceivers in the continuum of a Buddha are yogic direct perceivers. Some say that self-knowers and the five sense consciousnesses in a Buddha's continuum are omniscient consciousnesses. However, all omniscient consciousnesses must be yogic direct perceivers, and since all yogic direct perceivers are mental ones, a Buddha's sense consciousnesses could not possibly be yogic direct perceivers and thus could not be omniscient consciousnesses.

> These definitions are from the viewpoint of the Sautrāntikas. However, the Chittamātrins and the Yogāchāra- [Svātantrika]-Mādhyamikas give [as the definition of a direct perceiver] a non-conceptual knower arisen from stable predispositions.[36] [4a.3]

These systems agree that a direct perceiver must be free from conceptuality. However, in Chittamātra and Yogāchāra-Svātantrika-Mādhyamika, a direct perceiver does not have to be a non-mistaken knower because they assert that all sense and mental direct perceivers in the continuums of ordinary beings are mistaken with regard to their appearing objects in that when sounds, forms, and so forth appear to them, these appear to be external objects [but are not]. Moreover, tainted false aspectarian Chittamātrins[37] assert that not just ordinary beings, but even Buddhas have mistaken appearances. According to them, a Buddha's mode of understanding is not mistaken, but things still appear to a Buddha to be external objects.

Chittamātra also differs from Sautrāntika in its presentation of the three conditions: observed object, uncommon empowering, and immediately preceding conditions. Let us discuss the Sautrāntika presentation of these three first. The definition of the observed object condition of a sense direct perceiver apprehending a form is: 'that which principally and directly produces a sense direct perceiver apprehending a form as having the aspect of that form'.

The observed object condition of a sense direct perceiver apprehending a form is posited as the form itself because the consciousness is produced through the force of the form's casting its aspect to it. In other words, the form appears to it. The form is also posited as the observed object condition for a mental direct perceiver apprehending a form that is produced at the end of a continuum of sense direct perception.

An observed object condition is not posited for yogic and self-knowing direct perceivers, nor for conceptual consciousnesses. Although Pur-bu-jok in his *Collected Topics of Prime Cognition* does set forth an observed object condition for all of these, it seems that they must be only imputed ones and that his purpose in positing them must have been to sharpen students' reasoning and generate debate. The reason they must be only imputed is that to be an actual observed object condition, two features must be complete: the first is that it must appear to that mind, and the second is that the mind must be produced in dependence upon it. A yogic direct perceiver is produced in dependence upon a meditative stabilization which is a union of calm abiding and special insight. This meditative stabilization cannot be posited as its observed object condition because it does not appear to it. Also, in the case of a yogic direct perceiver realizing the selflessness of the person, one cannot posit the selflessness of the person as its observed object condition because in the Sautrāntika system the selflessness of the person, being a non-affirming negative (*prasajya-pratiṣhedha, med dgag*) and permanent, does not appear to a yogic direct perceiver. Even in the case of a yogic direct perceiver realizing impermanence with regard to an impermanent object which is appearing to it, one cannot say that it is produced in dependence on the object's casting its aspect to it; it is produced through the force of meditation. One can posit impermanence as its observed object (*ālambana-viṣhaya, dmigs yul*), but not as its observed object condition. Consciousnesses which depend upon an observed object condition are like old persons who must rely on a cane in order to stand up in that they depend on an object to give them their aspect. A yogic direct perceiver does not depend on its object in this manner.

One also cannot posit an observed object condition for a self-knowing direct perceiver, for as Jam-yang-shay-ba explains, an observed object condition is an appearance of a likeness of the object (*'dra rnam 'char ba gcig*) to the consciousness, and to a self-knower a likeness of the object does not appear since it is a consciousness for which there is no dualistic appearance.

Also for a thought consciousness there is no way to posit an observed object condition because what appears to a thought consciousness is a meaning generality which, being permanent, cannot be a *cause* of anything. Moreover, a thought consciousness is produced through the force not of an external object but of the consciousness which induces it, be that a prior moment of sense perception, memory, or whatever. Thus, observed object conditions are posited only for sense direct perceivers and the mental direct perceivers they induce.

The definition of an immediately preceding condition of a sense direct perceiver apprehending a form is: 'a knower which principally and directly produces a sense direct perceiver apprehending a form only as an experiencer which is a clear knower'.

An illustration of this is a consciousness which arises just immediately preceding a sense direct perceiver apprehending a form and which engages the mind in that form. This definition and illustration are applicable to all types of consciousnesses – mental direct perceivers, self-knowers, yogic direct perceivers, thought consciousnesses, and so forth.

The definition of the uncommon empowering condition of a sense direct perceiver apprehending a form is: 'that which principally and directly produces a sense direct perceiver apprehending a form as operating in its own sphere'.

An illustration is the clear inner form, the eye sense power, which is the uncommon empowering condition of a sense direct perceiver apprehending a form.

Anything which is a cause of a consciousness is necessarily an empowering condition of that consciousness; however, the *uncommon* empowering condition of a sense consciousness is only its respective sense power – the eye sense power for the eye consciousness, ear one for the ear consciousness, and so forth. In all tenet systems except Vaibhāṣhika one can say that a form appears to an eye sense power, but not that the sense power *sees* or *apprehends* the form. The Vaibhāṣhikas assert that an eye sense power also sees and apprehends forms.

For a mental direct perceiver apprehending a form, the uncommon empowering condition is a mental sense power which has become its own uncommon empowering condition. This qualifying phrase, 'which has become its own uncommon empowering condition', is necessary in order to eliminate a mental sense power which is simultaneous with the consciousness or after it – to specify just that mental sense power which is acting as its uncommon empowering condition. Because here the mental direct perceiver is apprehending a form, the eye sense power is its empowering condition though not its *uncommon empowering* condition which can only be a consciousness, in this case the last moment of the eye consciousness apprehending the form.

For a self-knowing direct perceiver the uncommon empowering condition is also a mental sense power which has become its own uncommon empowering condition. For a yogic direct perceiver it is a union of calm abiding and special insight which has become such.

When one posits these three conditions for a sense direct perceiver apprehending a form, one cannot say that they exist for only a single smallest moment (*dus mtha' skad cig ma*). However, with regard to mental direct perceivers in the continuums of ordinary beings apprehending forms, sounds, odours, and so forth, these three conditions exist for only one smallest moment and are thus very hidden phenomena. Once this is so, the observed object condition of a mental direct perceiver in the continuum of an ordinary being apprehending a form is a form which exists for only a smallest moment and thus is very hidden [accessible to ordinary beings only through scriptural inference]. However, having posited such a subtle form, it is impossible to say how that consciousness can realize it since a consciousness in the continuum of an ordinary being cannot realize a smallest moment, and it is for this reason that such mental direct perceivers are posited as awarenesses to which the object appears but is not ascertained.

Further, one can debate: Is whatever is a colour or shape necessarily an object of apprehension by an eye consciousness [colours and shapes being the twofold division of visible form, which is defined as 'object of apprehension by an eye consciousness']? If the opponent answers yes, one can posit the subject, the blue which is the observed object condition of a mental direct perceiver apprehending blue. This subject is a colour and thus must be an object of apprehension by an eye consciousness. One could then ask him if whatever is an object of apprehension by an eye consciousness is necessarily an object of realization by it. If he says yes, then it would absurdly follow that an eye consciousness would be able to realize the blue which is the observed object condition of a mental direct perceiver apprehending blue. This is not possible because this object is a very hidden phenomenon, and an eye consciousness in the continuum of an ordinary being is completely unable to realize very hidden phenomena, these being realized by common persons only in dependence on a reasoning process based on uncontradictible scriptures.

The preceding discussion of the three conditions has been

from the Sautrāntika viewpoint. The Chittamātra presentation differs significantly. In the latter's system, not objects but latent predispositions are posited as the observed object condition for both sense and mental direct perceivers. Thus, as the observed object condition of either a sense or mental direct perceiver apprehending a form the Chittamātrins posit a predisposition which exists with the immediately preceding condition of that consciousness and causes it to be generated as having the aspect of blue. The form which is apprehended by that sense or mental direct perceiver is called an *appearing* observed object condition. It is an observed object condition but not an actual one, called such because although it appears to the consciousness it does not produce it.

In the Chittamātra system, a form and the sense or mental direct perceiver apprehending it are one substantial entity and thus simultaneous, whereas an observed object condition must be a *cause* of a consciousness; whatever is a cause of something must be a different substantial entity from it and in a relationship of temporal sequence. If there were such an observed object condition, external objects would be entailed – this being impossible in the Chittamātra or Mind-Only system. In fact, the Sautrāntikas point to the existence of observed object conditions as establishing the existence of external objects.

The Sautrāntikas and Chittamātrins also differ in their presentation of the uncommon empowering conditions of sense and mental direct perceivers. Both agree that the uncommon empowering condition of, for example, an eye consciousness is the eye sense power and both call it form (*rūpa, gzugs*). However, for the Sautrāntikas this means that it is matter (*kanthā, bem po*), whereas for the Chittamātrins it is just a potency or power (*shakti, nus pa*). The latter say that it is a potency existing with the immediately preceding condition [a former moment of consciousness] and is a 'form' which produces a consciousness as having its own power, such as the eye consciousness having power with respect to colours and shapes. When this point is debated, it seems that in the end the

Chittamātrins do not assert any fully qualified forms once both internal forms [the uncommon empowering condition] and external ones [the observed object condition] are posited to be potencies. Thus, some earlier Tibetans said that the Chittamātra system does not have any fully qualified forms. However, after further analysis later scholars decided that it is not the case that there is in Chittamātra no fully qualified form; there is form – such as visible forms, sounds, odours, and so forth – but there is no matter since the definition of matter is that which is atomically established and in Chittamātra there are no externally existent atoms.

Now that we have discussed all four types of direct perceivers we should consider from what viewpoints this division is made, for in fact, all four can be included within a twofold division of sense and mental direct perceivers. There is nothing beyond these two, for the five sense direct perceivers – eye, ear, nose, tongue, and body ones – are included within sense direct perceivers, and mental, self-knowing, and yogic direct perceivers are all included within mental direct perceivers. Thus the question arises as to why direct perceivers are posited as four. Some scholars say that the reason is to clear away wrong ideas. For example, some non-Buddhists assert that all sense consciousnesses are conceptual; even within Buddhism, Prāsaṅgika asserts that some conceptual consciousnesses are direct perceivers. In order to eliminate these possibilities, the divisions are clearly expressed as four.

However, the main reason for positing four direct perceivers is from the viewpoint of their mode of production. Sense direct perceivers are those consciousnesses which are produced through the meeting of an object and a sense power. Yogic direct perceivers are produced through the force of meditation. Mental direct perceivers are produced either through the force of a former prime cognizer or through the force of meditation. Those produced through the force of former prime cognizers are mental direct perceivers apprehending visible forms, sounds, odours, tastes, and tangible objects. Those produced by the power of meditation are the five clairvoyances. Self-knowing direct perceivers are probably produced through the force of the consciousness which is its object of experience. This last explanation I have not seen in any book, but I feel that it is correct. A self-knowing direct perceiver is produced along with the consciousness that is its object of experience, and once this is the case, one can say that it is produced through the force of the consciousness which is its object of experience. Thus, one can explain four direct perceivers as being posited both for the sake of clearing away wrong ideas and from the viewpoint of their mode of production.

Ge-shay Jam-bel-sam-pel will now explain ancillarily the topic of facsimiles of direct perception (*pratyakṣha-ābhāsa, mngon sum ltar snang*) which are so-called because while not actual direct perceivers, they appear to be like them. Seven types of facsimiles of direct perception are described – six conceptual and one non-conceptual, into which all types of thought can be included.

> Ancillarily, with respect to briefly explaining the presentation of facsimiles of direct perceivers, [Dignāga's *Compendium on Prime Cognition*] says: 'Mistaken [conception], conventional consciousness, inferential [conception], [conception] arise from inference, memory-[conception], and wishing-[conception] are facsimiles of direct perception along with dimness of sight.'
>
> Thus, seven facsimiles of direct perception are asserted: six conceptual and one non-conceptual. [4a. 3–4b.1]

A mistaken conception is, for example, a wrong conceptual consciousness such as a thought apprehending sound to be permanent. An instance of a conventional conception is an inferential cognizer realizing sound to be impermanent.

An inferential conception is a consciousness which is a mind apprehending a sign. For instance, there is a correct opponent who is a ground for establishing sound to be impermanent, that is, who is about to realize that sound is impermanent, and in this person's continuum there is a consciousness that realizes the three modes (*trirūpa, tshul gsum*) in the proof of sound as impermanent. It has realized the presence of the reason in the subject (*pakṣha-dharma, phyogs chos*), the pervasion (*anvaya-vyāpti, rjes khyab*) and the counter-pervasion (*vyatireka-vyāpti, ldog khyab*). Such a consciousness realizing the three modes is called a consciousness which has become a mind apprehending the sign (**liṅga-grahana-chitta, rtags 'dzin sems*) and is an instance of an inferential conception within this sevenfold division of facsimiles of direct perception. It is not an actual inferential cognizer but will in the next moment become one.

A conception arisen from inference is, for example, a consciousness which arises subsequent to an inferential cognizer, such as a remembering consciousness induced by an inferential cognizer – i.e., the memory one has after an inference.

A memory-conception is, for example, a consciousness remembering today something that happened in the past. A wishing-conception is, for example, a consciousness wishing in the present for something in the future.

Those are the six conceptual facsimiles of direct perceivers. With regard to the non-conceptual one, Dignāga's stating of 'dimness of sight' refers to that which is seen by a person who has an eye disease causing him to see hairs falling in front of him. This indicates by extension all non-conceptual wrong consciousnesses.

> In the root text of Dharmakīrti's *Commentary on (Dignāga's) 'Compendium on Prime Cognition'* these are condensed into four. If you wish to know about these in more detail, please look in the Ra-dö (*Rva-stod*) *Awareness and Knowledge* and in [Pan-chen Sö-nam-drak-ba's] *Illumination of the Thought* on the third chapter [of Dharmakīrti's *Commentary on (Dignāga's) 'Compendium on Prime Cognition'*] and so forth. [4b.1]

Dharmakīrti explains these seven facsimiles of direct perception by means of a fourfold division:

1 conceptions having a term as their basis (*brda' rten can gyi rtog pa*)
2 conceptions making superimpositions on other objects (*don gzhan la sgro 'dogs pa'i rtog pa*)

3 conceptions having a hidden object (*lkog tu gyur pa'i don can gyi rtog pa*)
4 non-conceptual facsimiles of direct perception (*rtog med mngon sum ltar snang*)

The first of these four, conceptions possessing a term as their basis, includes all factually concordant conceptual consciousnesses except for inferential cognizers and the consciousnesses they induce. Thus, from Dignāga's list of seven facsimiles of direct perception, memory-conceptions and wishing-conceptions are included in it. Conceptions making superimpositions on other objects refer to wrong thought consciousnesses; thus from the seven fold listing, it includes within it the first, wrong conceptions. Conceptions having a hidden object refer to inferential cognizers and the consciousnesses they induce; thus from Dignāgā's list it includes conventional conceptions, inferential conceptions, and conceptions arisen from inference. Non-conceptual facsimiles of direct perception are the same in both lists.

3. *Inferential and Subsequent Cognizers*

Inferential cognizers

The definition of an inferential cognizer is a determinative knower which, depending on its basis, a correct sign, is incontrovertible with regard to its object of comprehension, a hidden phenomenon. [4b. 2]

The Sautrāntikas following reasoning, Chittamātrins, and Svātantrika-Mādhyamikas assert that all inferential cognizers must be produced in dependence on a basis that is a correct sign. Within Prāsaṅgika, some textbooks say that this is not necessarily the case, for although those of dull faculties can generate an inference only in dependence on a correct sign, those of sharpest faculties can generate one merely in dependence on a consequence (*prasaṅga, thal 'gyur*).[38] Other textbooks on Prāsaṅgika which say that an inferential cognizer can only be produced in dependence on a correct sign respond that while it is not necessary explicitly to state a correct reason to a practitioner of sharpest faculties, that person would think one out for himself, and thus his inferential consciousness is produced in dependence on a correct sign. In any case, they are called Prāsaṅgikas – Consequentialists – because they assert that an inference can be generated merely by the statement of a consequence. It is helpful to think over both sides of this issue.

The meaning of 'correct sign' is discussed extensively in the study of 'Signs and Reasonings' (*rtags rigs*). However, in brief, correct sign means correct reason (*samyak-nimitta, rgyu mtshan yang dag*), correct reasoning (*samyak-nyāya, rigs pa yang dag*), or correct proof (*samyak-sādhana, sgrub byed yang dag*). A mind which realizes its object of comprehension in dependence on such is called an inferential cognizer.

That an inferential cognizer is 'incontrovertible' means that it realizes its object – it attains, gets at, an object with respect to which superimpositions have been removed. It is a determinative knower, that is, it is a consciousness for which there is a sense, 'It is such and such,' which does not occur for sense consciousnesses or other direct perceivers, but only for thought. Inferential cognizers are so-called because of being inferring consciousnesses which arise in dependence on a correct sign or reason.

> The definition of an inferential prime cognizer is a determinative knower which, depending on its basis, a correct sign, is new and incontrovertible with regard to its object of comprehension, a hidden phenomenon. It is said that an inferential cognizer is not necessarily a prime cognizer. [4b. 2–3]

Thus, in this text there is a distinction between inferential cognizer and inferential prime cognizer. In other texts, for instance, Pur-bu-jok's *Awareness and Knowledge*, this distinction is not made; the two are considered synonymous. Here it is asserted that there are three possibilities between the two in that all inferential prime cognizers are inferential cognizers but there are inferential cognizers which are not prime, such as the second moment of an inferential cognizer realizing sound to be impermanent. Such a consciousness is an inferential cognizer but not prime, new. Rather, it is an inference which is a subsequent cognizer.

Because Pur-bu-jok asserts that all inferential cognizers are prime, he does not accept a common locus of a subsequent cognizer and an inferential cognizer. Thus, for him the second moment of an inferential cognizer is no longer an inferential cognizer but is just a subsequent one. It is a conceptual remembering consciousness. Pur-bu-jok's position is also asserted by Jay-dzun-ba (*rJe-rtsun-pa, rJe-rtsun Chos-kyi-rgyal-mtshan*, 1469–

1546), author of the textbooks for the Jay College of Se-ra Monastery, whereas Pan-chen Sö-nam-drak-ba's assertion accords with our text. When this text says, '*It is said* that an inferential cognizer is not necessarily a prime cognizer', it is referring to him.

When inferential cognizers are divided, there are three:
1 inference through belief (**āpta-anumāna, yid ches rjes dpag)*
2 inference through renown (**prasiddha-anumāna, grags pa'i rjes dpag)*
3 inference by the power of the fact (**vastu-bala-anumāna, dugos stobs rjes dpag)* [4b.3]

This is a division of inferential cognizers by way of their entities.

The definition of an inferential cognizer through belief is a determinative knower which, depending on its basis, a correct sign of belief, is incontrovertible with regard to its object of comprehension, a very hidden phenomenon. An illustration is the inferential consciousness which realizes that the scripture, 'From giving, resources; from ethics, a happy [migration]', is incontrovertible with respect to the meaning indicated by it. [4b.3–4]

Thus, an inferential cognizer through belief is one which has as its basis a sign of belief, a sign that is believed in, in dependence on which one realizes a very hidden object of comprehension. With regard to the illustration cited here, the scripture is saying that from engaging in giving, a person comes to have resources, and from maintaining pure ethics, a person attains a happy migration. However, one does not need inference through belief to realize just that through giving resources are achieved, for this is not a very hidden phenomenon; to realize the very hidden phenomena such as the specific action of giving, its entity, its object, the giver, the time of giving, and so forth involved in the arising of a specific resource, one needs inference through belief. With regard to the statement, 'From ethics, a happy migration', what is being realized is a specific entity of ethics, what one avoided, with respect to whom one kept ethics, the time of keeping it, the keeper, and so forth. All these can be realized only through an inference through belief as they are very hidden phenomena.

Such a scripture is 'incontrovertible with respect to the meaning indicated by it' in that the meaning of the scripture is definite as just what it says. One realizes this incontrovertibility by means of a sign of belief. What such a sign is can be understood through stating the above illustration in syllogistic form: The subject, the scripture, 'From giving, resources; from ethics, a happy migration,' is incontrovertible with respect to the meaning indicated by it because of being a scripture free from the three contradictions. The sign of belief – the reason believed in – is that the scripture is free from the three contradictions. To be free from such means that the scripture is not damaged, or harmed, by the three prime cognizers: direct prime cognizer, inference by the power of the fact, and inference through belief. These are consciousnesses realizing the three types of objects of comprehension:

1 the manifest (*abhimukhī, mngon gyur*)
2 slightly hidden (*kimcid-parokṣha, cung zad lkog gyur*)
3 very hidden *atyartha-parokṣha, shin tu lkog gyur*)

The manifest are those things which can be seen with ordinary direct perception. The slightly hidden are those which must be established for common beings in dependence on a sign by the power of the fact, such as liberation and omniscience, the selflessness of the person, the subtle impermanence of sound, and so forth. Very hidden phenomena are such things as the subtle features of the cause and effect of actions, as taught in the scripture, 'Through giving, resources,' where the object given, the recipient of the gift, the giver, the time of giving, and so forth [leading to a specific resource] are all very hidden phenomena. These are accessible to inference, but only that through belief, which is also called scriptural inference.

There is a great deal of debate as to whether or not a specific scripture, if it is free from the three contradictions, has to teach all three objects of comprehension. Scripture in general teaches the three types, but most individual scriptures do not teach all three. Thus, there are two ways of positing something as free from the three contradictions: one can say either that it is free from contradiction 'with respect to its teaching the perceivable manifest' or 'with respect to that part which teaches the perceivable manifest'. Pan-chen Sö-nam-drak-ba and Kay-drub Rin-bo-chay use the first; Jay-dzun-ba uses the second.

Following the first, to be free from the three contradictions means: 'With respect to its teaching of the perceivable manifest, it is not damaged by a direct prime cognizer. With respect to its teaching of the slightly hidden, it is not damaged by an inference by the power of the fact. With respect to its teaching of the very hidden, it is not damaged by an inference through belief.'

Following the second form, this statement would be phrased, 'With respect to that part which teaches the perceivable manifest, it is not damaged by a direct prime cognizer', and so forth. Kay-drub Rin-bo-chay and Pan-chen Sö-nam-drak-ba find fault with this form, for they say such wording implies that a scripture free from the three contradictions must teach all three objects of comprehension, whereas this is not the case, since some scriptures teach only one of them. However, those who say 'that part which teaches' respond that this is said not with reference to all particular scriptures, but to scripture in general. This is all right from the viewpoint of understanding but is rather difficult to hold in debate.

Basically, the meaning of being free from the three contradictions is: 'If the passage teaches the perceivable manifest, there is no damage by a direct prime cognizer. If it teaches the slightly hidden, there is no damage by an inference by the power of the fact. If it teaches the very hidden, there is no damage by an inference through belief.' For example, if it is teaching about water and says that it runs uphill, there is contradiction by direct perception. If it teaches the slightly hidden and says that persons possess substantial existence, this is damaged by inference by the power of the fact. If it teaches a very hidden topic such as saying that happy migrations arise from giving [whereas they actually arise from ethics], that is damaged by inference through belief – by another scripture which teaches a very hidden phenomenon [i.e., that resources arise from giving]. Scriptures which are not damaged in any of these ways are said to be free from the three contradictions.

> The definition of an inferential cognizer through renown is a determinative knower which, depending on its basis, a correct sign of renown, is incontrovertible with respect to its object of comprehension, a terminological suitability. An illustration is the inferential consciousness that realizes it is suitable to express the rabbit-possessor by the term 'moon'. [4b.4–5a.1]

All consciousnesses are produced in dependence on a basis; the basis for this type of inference is a sign of renown. In other words, it operates on an object which is established through the power of renown in the world. The illustration given above stated in syllogistic form would be 'The subject, the rabbit-possessor [a name for the moon], is suitable to be expressed with the term "moon" because of existing among objects of thought.' A similar statement can be made with regard to anything – 'The subject, John, is suitable to be expressed with the term "moon" because of existing among objects of thought.' In other words, it is suitable to call John anything – moon, sun, or any other name one wants to designate to him, and thus in Tibet children were often given names such as Buddha, Giving, Ethics, Patience, Effort, Wisdom, and so forth. Also, it is suitable to change names.

The reason for this suitability of expression is simply the subject's existing among objects of thought. Any object that can be thought of is suitable to be designated with any name. Whatever one wants to call an object is all right because names do not inhere in objects.

One can understand this through the example 'pot', the name designated to a bulbous flat-based water holder. A bulbous thing's being a 'pot' is not something which is established as its own mode of being from its mere production.

Rather, someone initially affixed the name, the verbal convention, 'pot', to a bulbous flat-based water holder, and this came to be renowned as its actual name. However, one could just as easily call it something else – for instance, 'woollen cloth', and in time, with repeated usage, when one said 'woollen cloth', the image appearing to one's mind would be that of a bulbous flat-based water holder. The fact that now when we say 'pot' a bulbous flat-based water holder appears to our minds and when we say 'woollen cloth' a fabric woven from sheep's wool appears is merely by the power of the predispositions of expression – those predispositions established by our usage of expressions. It is not by the power of the external object but by that of association, and this association can be changed. This is not the case with qualities inhering in an object; for example, to a direct perceiver apprehending a fire, the hot and burning appears and the wet and moistening – the qualities of water – do not. This is because heat abides as the nature of fire.

An inference through renown is a consciousness realizing that it is suitable to express an object with a term just because it exists among objects of thought. Such a consciousness is incontrovertible with respect to its object of comprehension, a terminological suitability. In the instance cited, rabbit-possessor itself is not a terminological suitability, but the suitability of expressing the rabbit-possessor with the term moon is one. The reason that the example is stated as it is – that the rabbit-possessor is suitable to be called the moon, rather than saying that the moon is suitable to be called the rabbit-possessor – is that there are many different objects designated by the term 'moon' – quicksilver, a young girl's face, camphor, a kind of medicine, and the orb in the night sky. The point being made is that because the moon exists among objects of thought, it can be called anything.

The definition of an inferential consciousness by the power of the fact is a determinative knower which depending on its basis, a correct sign by the power of the fact, is incontrovertible with

> respect to its object of comprehension, a slightly hidden phenomenon. An illustration is the inferential consciousness which realizes that sound is impermanent. [5a.1–2]

In this type of inference, the basis of the consciousness is a correct sign by the power of the fact, this being a reason which proves a slightly hidden phenomenon. Because an inferential cognizer by the power of the fact comprehends a meaning that abides in the object – the thing itself – it understands an object which is established by the power of the thing itself. In general, there are two types of objects: those established by the power of the thing itself and those established by the power of renown. With regard to the first, hot and burning resides in the 'thingness' of fire, in the nature of fire. Another way of saying this is that hot and burning really exist with fire. When one touches fire, no aspect other than that of hot and burning appears, and thus, the hot and burning is called an object that is established by the power of the thing. One can call fire the 'cleaner' or the 'crested', but its being these is not established by the power of the thing. Pigs are also cleaners and peacocks are renowned as crested; thus 'cleaner' and 'crested' are just objects established by the power of renown in relation to fire.

One can take a sound as an example. The fact that it is produced or established as definite to disintegrate moment by moment right from the time of its own production is the mode of subsistence of sound. Therefore, even Buddhas and Bodhisattvas who have inconceivable powers such as turning earth into gold do not have the power to change sound from being definite to disintegrate moment by moment into not so disintegrating. Therefore, an inference which realizes that sound is impermanent comprehends that fact through the force of the sound's being established in its own actuality as impermanent.

This threefold division of inferential cognizers into those through belief, renown, and the power of the fact is made by way of their entities. If one makes a division by way of their mode of production, there are two: prime and subsequent.

There is no such thing as an inferential cognizer that is an awareness to which an object appears but is not ascertained, since it must realize its object.

There is also a terminological twofold division of inferential cognizers into inference for oneself (*svārtha-anumāna, rang don rjes dpag*) and for another (*parārtha-anumāna, gzhan don rjes dpag*). That for oneself refers to inference as has been set forth above in its threefold division by way of entity. That for another refers to a proof statement, which is posited before the statement of a reason. First a consequence is stated, then a proof statement, and then a reason. This division is terminological because whatever is an inference must be a consciousness, and inference for another, being a proof statement, is sound – matter – and not consciousness. Thus, whatever is an actual inference is necessarily an inference for oneself.

The use of inference for another is as follows. In order to overcome the wrong view of, for instance, a Sāṃkhya who asserts that sound is permanent, one would first state a consequence: It follows that the subject, sound, is not a product because of being permanent. This should cause him to become doubtful, whereupon it is necessary to establish for him the three modes: the presence of the reason in the subject, the pervasion, and the counter-pervasion. To establish the first, one would posit, 'The subject, sound, is a product because of being a created thing.' This proves the presence of the reason in the subject – that sound is a product. To establish the positive pervasion, one would state, 'The subject, a product, is impermanent because of being momentary.' By explicitly proving the pervasion, one implicitly proves the counter-pervasion.

Having established the three modes, one then makes a proof statement. The person has realized individually the presence of the reason in the subject, the positive pervasion, and the counter-pervasion; a proof statement is given in order that all three might appear simultaneously to his mind. One states, 'Whatever is a product is necessarily impermanent – for example, a pot. Sound is also a product.' If one proof statement will suffice, then it can be left at this. If two are necessary, then one would say, 'Whatever is permanent is necessarily not a product – for example, uncaused space. Sound, however, is a product.' The positing of one or two proof statements is done in dependence on the sharpness or dullness of faculties of the person to whom these are being posited. To a person of sharp faculties one first posits a consequence and establishes the presence of the reason in the subject and so forth. Then it may or may not be necessary to posit even one proof statement, but at the most one will suffice. Then at the end one states to him a reason – for example, the syllogism, 'The subject, sound, is impermanent because of being a product.' To a person of dull faculties, a consequence, two proof statements, and a reason must be stated.

When we debate, we do not usually go through this entire process. We proceed as though the three modes were established and the opponent were of sharp faculties. However, if one were doing it very carefully, all those steps would be used. Still, there are some to whom it is not necessary to state a consequence, for example, those who do not have a previous wrong idea. Hence, in establishing to a Buddhist the impermanence of sound, it is not necessary to state a consequence as he has no previous wrong view that sound is permanent. However, for a Sāṃkhya, who does have this wrong view, it is necessary to go through all these stages. Though our textbooks often present our own system in the form of consequential statements, this is not that the students have actual wrong views to be eliminated; rather, these are used because there is some doubt as to whether the students are quite ready for syllogistic statements.

Subsequent cognizers

The definition of a subsequent cognizer is a knower which is not a prime cognizer and which realizes what has already been realized by the former prime cognizer inducing it. [5a.2–3]

There is some problem with this definition as it is stated because a subsequent cognizer is a positive phenomenon and the definition is a negative phenomenon due to the fact that it says, 'is not a prime cognizer'. To avoid this problem, most other presentations of 'Awareness and Knowledge' posit as the definition of subsequent cognizer: 'a knower which realizes that which has already been realized'.

I find this definition preferable. There is also some difficulty in the first definition with the part that says 'by the former prime cognizer inducing it', as will become clear later when the divisions of subsequent cognizers are explained.

> When subsequent cognizers are divided, there are two: direct (**pratyakṣha-parichchhinna-jñāna, mngon sum bcad shes*) and conceptual subsequent cognizers (**kalpanā-parichchhinna-jñāna, rtog pa bcad shes*). There are four direct subsequent cognizers: sense, mental, self-knowing, and yogic. [5a.3–4]

A sense direct subsequent cognizer is, for example, the second moment of a sense direct perceiver apprehending a form. An example of a mental direct one is the second moment of a mental perceiver in the continuum of a Superior which is apprehending a form. There is no such subsequent cognizer in the continuum of an ordinary being because mental direct perceivers apprehending forms and so forth are only one smallest moment and thus for ordinary beings are awarenesses to which an object appears but is not ascertained. A mental subsequent cognizer which does exist in the continuums of some ordinary beings is the second moment of a clairvoyant consciousness knowing another's mind. An example of a self-knowing subsequent cognizer is the second moment of a self-knower which is experiencing a sense direct perceiver apprehending a form. An example of a yogic subsequent cognizer is the second moment of a yogic direct perceiver directly realizing the selflessness of the person.

> There are two conceptual subsequent cognizers: those induced by direct perception and those induced by inference. An illustration of a conceptual subsequent cognizer induced by direct perception is a consciousness ascertaining blue which is produced subsequent to a direct perceiver apprehending blue; an illustration

of a conceptual subsequent cognizer induced by inference is the second moment of an inferential consciousness that realizes sound to be impermanent.[39] [5a.4–5b.1]

In the case of a conceptual subsequent cognizer induced by direct perception, a sense direct perceiver apprehending blue sees the blue, and subsequent to that the thought is induced, 'I saw blue.' In the case of a conceptual subsequent cognizer induced by inference, the first moment of an inferential cognizer realizing sound to be impermanent, itself a conceptual consciousness, induces a second moment of inference which realizes sound to be impermanent; that second moment is a conceptual subsequent cognizer induced by inference.

This is because it says in Ḍharmottara's *The Correct* (*'Thad-ldan*),[40] 'The two – the first moment of a direct perceiver or of an inferential consciousness – are prime cognizers, but later moments which do not differ in establishment and abiding and are continuations of them have forsaken being prime cognizers'. Sameness in establishment and abiding on this occasion is said to refer to sameness of effect. [5b.1–2]

The first moment of a direct perceiver refers to, for example, the first moment of any of the five sense direct perceivers – those apprehending forms, sounds, odours, tastes, or tangible objects. The first moment of any direct perceiver which is not an awareness to which an object appears but is not ascertained or the first moment of any inferential cognizer is a prime cognizer. Later moments within the same continuum of consciousness, that is, later moments which are not different from the first in establishment and abiding, are no longer prime cognizers; they are subsequent cognizers. The sameness of effect that is to be understood as the meaning of 'sameness in establishment and abiding' refers to the generation of a common effect by the moments of consciousness; for example, the first and second moments of an eye consciousness apprehending blue generate as their common effect a consciousness ascertaining the blue – one able to remember that blue has been seen.

In one sense, because objects are new in each moment, each moment of a consciousness could be said to be realizing a new object. However, this is not the meaning of the 'new' which serves as the basis for distinguishing prime and subsequent cognizers. The first moment of a consciousness engages an object *by its own power*, whereas subsequent moments realize their objects merely by the force of the former prime cognizer that induced them, and thus the first moment is a prime cognizer and later ones are subsequent cognizers.

The assertion is that the first moment of direct perceivers and of inferential cognizers are prime cognizers and all subsequent moments – the second, third, fourth, fifth, and so on, however many there are – within the same continuum of consciousness are subsequent cognizers. This is true in the case of sense, mental, self-knowing, and – in the continuums of Learner Superiors – yogic direct perceivers. However, it is not suitable to posit this with regard to omniscient consciousnesses – exalted knowers of all aspects (*sarvākārajñāna, rnam mkhyen*) – for Gyel-tsap, Kay-drup, and all the textbooks say that whatever is an omniscient consciousness is necessarily a prime cognizer. For example, Kay-drup's *Clearing Away Darkness of Mind with Respect to the Seven Treatises* says, 'I do not feel that whatever is an omniscient consciousness is not necessarily a prime cognizer or that whatever is a prime cognizer is not necessarily a new realizer.' In other words, an omniscient consciousness is necessarily a prime cognizer, and a prime cognizer is necessarily a new realizer. In brief, an omniscient consciousness is never a subsequent cognizer.

One could debate this assertion that all omniscient consciousnesses are prime cognizers and, taking as one's subject the second moment of an omniscient consciousness, say, 'The subject, the second moment of an omniscient consciousness, is a subsequent cognizer because of engaging an object which was already realized by the first moment of the omniscient consciousness.' It is with the intention of preventing such a debate that the definition in this text specifies a subsequent cognizer as 'a knower which is not a prime cognizer'. The author is willing to accept that the second moment of an omniscient consciousness does engage the objects realized by its first moment, but nonetheless asserts that it is a prime cognizer because an omniscient consciousness always operates *under its own power* and not through the force of having been induced by a previous moment of prime cognition. He avoids having to call it a subsequent cognizer by defining subsequent cognizers as necessarily non-prime cognizers.

Many other texts define a subsequent cognizer as a knower realizing that which has already been realized. They explain this as meaning a knower that engages an object *which has already been realized by the former prime cognizer which induced it* and not merely as meaning that which engages an object that has already been realized as the words of the definition would seem to indicate. This distinction is also made to avoid having to call the second moment of an omniscient consciousness a subsequent cognizer. For, the second moment of an omniscient consciousness engages an object by its own power without being induced by a former prime cognizer and without having to depend on the activity of a memory-consciousness.

Moreover, there are many qualities simultaneous with the first moment of an omniscient consciousness, and many simultaneous with its second moment. The second moment of an omniscient consciousness, in realizing those qualities which are simultaneous with the first moment, realizes that which has already been realized by the first moment, but it is newly realizing those qualities which are simultaneous with it. Thus, Jam-yang-shay-ba and most other textbook authors say that the second, third, fourth, fifth, and however many moments there are of an omniscient consciousness are prime cognizers because they newly realize those qualities which are simultaneous with them.

With regard to, for example, a mind realizing sound to be impermanent, the first moment of initial generation of an inferential cognizer of such is a prime cognizer. Subsequent moments of it as well as later occasions of taking this realization to mind are, up to the point of attaining calm abiding with respect to the impermanence of sound, subsequent cognizers that are arisen from thought. With the achievement of such calm abiding, one must continue repeatedly to take this to mind, to cultivate it within calm abiding for the sake of attaining a clear appearance of the impermanence of sound. Until clear appearance is attained, all those awarenesses taking to mind the impermanence of sound within calm abiding are subsequent cognizers which are states arisen from meditation. When clear appearance is attained, that is, when the impermanence of sound is initially realized directly, one again has a prime cognizer – the first moment of direct perception of the impermanence of sound. Even though it arises by the power of the former moments of realization, it does not arise through the force of former moments *of direct perception*. Because it is in this sense a new realization, it is a prime cognizer. All succeeding moments, however many there may be, are subsequent cognizers.

There is much debate as to whether, if one gets up from one's meditative session and some time later returns to meditation on the same topic, the first moment of direct perception is again a prime cognizer or is still a subsequent one. Some say that it is prime because one is newly generating a continuum of direct perception; others say that it is not a prime cognizer because it is engaging its object due to the force of the former direct perception. From the viewpoint that one is familiarizing with what has already been seen, it would seem to be a subsequent cognizer; however, from the viewpoint that it is a new awareness engaging a new object, it would seem to be a prime cognizer. Both views can be argued persuasively. There are also some who say that there are no yogic direct perceivers which are subsequent cognizers because all must be prime cognizers.

My own thought is that if one is continuously meditating on an object such as the impermanence of sound, the first moment of direct perception is a prime cognizer and all subsequent moments within that specific continuum of meditation are subsequent cognizers. If one leaves the meditation for some time and later returns to it, again newly and directly realizing one's object of meditation, the first moment of direct perception is again a prime cognizer and all subsequent moments within that continuum of meditation are again subsequent cognizers. This is, I feel, not the same as an omniscient consciousness. It engages its object due to the force of having removed the two obstructions – to liberation and to omniscience – and thus engages objects through its own force, not through the force of prior moments of realization. On the paths of learning, although one may have yogic direct perception, one has not removed the two obstructions, and thus there is not this same ability to engage objects through its own force. I feel that in this regard a yogic direct perceiver is not like an omniscient consciousness, and thus although all omniscient consciousnesses are prime cognizers, yogic direct perceivers can be both prime and subsequent cognizers.

Other textbooks use a different syllable as the first part of the Tibetan term for subsequent cognizer, using *dpyad*, analysis, instead of *bcad*, eliminated. Those using 'eliminated' say that 'analysis' is incorrect with regard to sense direct perceivers which are non-conceptual and thus do not have any activity of analysis. I agree with this view, for sense direct perceivers are not analytical consciousnesses; I thus feel that one should use the syllable meaning 'eliminated' because even direct subsequent cognizers do eliminate superimpositions with respect to their objects in that at the time of perceiving, for example, blue one eliminates the superimposition of non-blue. This does not mean that one is explicitly thinking, 'This is not green,' for there is no thought involved in direct perception. However, the mere fact that one's eye consciousness engages a blue object correctly means that one will not think, 'This is green,' and in this sense a superimposition has been eliminated. There is also a conceptual elimination of superimpositions which occurs in states arisen from thought (*chintāmayī*, *bsam byung*) and in states of special insight – such as eliminating the superimposition of a self of persons at the time of realizing the selflessness of persons. Though the elimination of superimpositions which takes place in direct perception is not like that, direct perceivers are consciousnesses which *realize* their objects and thus are incontrovertible with respect to their objects. To be incontrovertible means that a consciousness has gotten at an object with respect to which superimpositions have been eliminated. Thus, if a consciousness did not eliminate superimpositions with respect to its object, it could not get at that object and could not realize it. Therefore, I feel that one must posit direct perceivers' mere engagement of an object as an elimination of superimpositions, for direct perceivers can realize their objects and be incontrovertible in the sense of not being susceptible to contradiction by other prime cognizers.

The three types of consciousnesses that have been discussed up to this point – direct perceivers, inferential cognizers, and subsequent cognizers – are all awarenesses which realize their objects [except for those direct perceivers that are awarenesses to which an object appears but is not ascertained]. Remaining to be discussed among the division of awarenesses and knowers into seven are correctly assuming consciousnesses, awarenesses to which an object appears but is not ascertained, doubting consciousnesses, and wrong consciousnesses. These four are all awarenesses which never realize their objects.

4. *Non-Cognizing Awarenesses*

Correctly assuming consciousnesses

The definition of a correctly assuming consciousness is a knower that does not get at an object with respect to which superimpositions have been eliminated although it adheres one-pointedly to the phenomenon which is its principal object of engagement [5b.2–3]

A correctly assuming consciousness is, for example, the knowledge that arises when something is explained to you. At such a time, there is first generated an ear consciousness hearing what was said, and it then induces an awareness thinking, 'It is such and such.' That awareness – which is based only on a sound generality – is a correctly assuming consciousness. For example, if someone is explaining to you a presentation of 'Awareness and Knowledge', and you think, 'This is direct perception, that is inference,' and so forth, your understanding is correct assumption. Should you then think about it again and again and finally ascertain it decisively in dependence on a correct sign, that mind would be an inferential prime cognizer. However, states prior to that point as you are still thinking about it and seeking to increase your understanding are all correctly assuming consciousnesses.

Not all consciousnesses arisen from hearing (*shrutamayī, thos byung*) are correctly assuming ones; for example, if someone tells you that sound is permanent and you generate a consciousness assenting to this statement, you would have generated a wrong consciousness. Any *wisdom* arisen from hearing (*shrutamayī-prajñā, thos byung gi shes rab*), however, is a correctly assuming consciousness.

Such an awareness is a knower which determines one-pointedly, or decisively, the phenomenon which is its main object of engagement. The main object of engagement of, for example, a correctly assuming consciousness realizing the impermanence of sound is the impermanence of sound. The consciousness one-pointedly thinks, 'Sound is impermanent.' However, it does not get at an object with respect to which superimpositions have been eliminated, or does not eliminate false superimpositions with respect to its object, and thus it does not *realize* its object. It apprehends, ascertains, and is mindful of its object, but does not realize it.

Some posit a different definition for a correctly assuming consciousness: 'a controvertible factually concordant determinative knower that determines its own object'.

However, to refute this definition, one can put forth the following subject: an awareness which, wondering whether sound is permanent or impermanent, thinks that it is probably impermanent. This subject is a doubting consciousness, but it fulfills this definition of a correctly assuming consciousness. It determines its object because it is a conceptual consciousness and all conceptual consciousnesses do this in that all have the conceptual element of thinking, 'It is such and such.' It is controvertible, for it does not realize its object. It is a conceptual consciousness – not a direct perceiver. It is factually concordant, because it is correct; it thinks that sound is impermanent as it is. The fault with this definition is that it does not specify that a correctly assuming consciousness determines its object decisively, in a one-pointed manner, not having the vacillation, or two-pointedness, of doubt.

Another definition that some posit for a correctly assuming consciousness is: 'a conceptual knower that newly and one-pointedly ascertains its own true object without depending on either experience or a correct sign which is its basis'.

This is how it is given in the Ra-dö *Awareness and Knowledge* and others. However, this definition is difficult to hold in debate, as it is not the case that whatever is a correctly assuming consciousness does not depend on either experience or a correct sign.

Experience is of three types: that of direct perception, of self-knowing, and that which is arisen from meditation. Direct perception always occurs within the context of experience for when a direct perceiver realizes an object, it does so by the power of experience. A self-knower experiences the consciousness which is its object, with which it is one substantial entity undifferentiable in establishment and abiding. Experience which is arisen from meditation is attained with calm abiding. There are other ways of positing and discussing experience, but this threefold division is the referent in this definition of a correctly assuming consciousness.

Those who object to the above definition posit the subject, a correctly assuming consciousness which is an effect of experience.[41] It does depend on experience and thus is not a consciousness which, as specified in the definition, does not depend on either experience or a correct sign. Although the sense in which it depends on experience is none of the three types listed above, since it does depend on experience, it cannot – according to the above definition – be a correctly assuming consciousness.

According to this definition, a correctly assuming consciousness also does not depend on a correct sign which is its basis. 'Correct sign' refers to the three types of signs mentioned in the discussion of inferential cognizers: those of belief, by the power of the fact, or of renown. Basically this means that a correctly assuming consciousness cannot depend on a correct reason, for any consciousness which does so is necessarily an inferential cognizer, a mind which realizes its object. Such cognition is firm, stable; once something has been realized with inference, one will not change from what one has ascertained as long as it is remembered. Correctly assuming consciousnesses, on the other hand, lack this stability. Being consciousnesses which are merely assertions, merely beliefs,

direct perceivers, whatever is the main object of operation is necessarily the appearing object; however, whatever is its object of engagement is not necessarily its appearing object – for one can say that the opposite from non-form is its object of engagement but not that such appears to it.

Also, whatever is an appearing object of a direct perceiver is not necessarily its object of engagement, because the impermanence of the form, its momentariness, the form's ability to perform a function, and so forth are all appearing objects of a direct perceiver apprehending a form but not objects of engagement. This is true even in the case of a sense direct perceiver in the continuum of a Superior apprehending a form.

In the case of a non-conceptual wrong consciousness such as a sense consciousness perceiving white snow mountains as blue, there are appearing and apprehended objects but no object of engagement or determined object. If one were asked to posit the object of engagement of such a mind, one would have to posit blue snow mountains – which do not exist, and thus one answers that the object of engagement does not exist. This distinction is important in terms of the definition of an awareness to which an object appears but is not ascertained as will be discussed later. One cannot posit a determined object for non-conceptual wrong consciousnesses because only thought consciousnesses have such.

That is the manner in which the four types of objects are applied to different types of consciousnesses. In general, one can say that whatever is an established base is necessarily all four objects – a determined object, object of engagement, appearing object, and apprehended object. For, any phenomenon is necessarily the determined object and the object of engagement of the thought apprehending it. Also, whatever is permanent is necessarily the appearing and the apprehended object of the thought apprehending it, and whatever is an impermanent thing is necessarily the appearing and apprehended object of the direct perceiver apprehending it. This stems from the basic Sautrāntika assertion that appearing object of thought and permanent phenomenon are synonymous, and appearing object of direct perception and impermanent thing are synonymous.

Returning to the definition of an awareness to which the object appears but is not ascertained, it is defined as: 'a knower to which the specifically characterized phenomenon which is its object of engagement clearly appears but which is unable to induce ascertainment with respect to it'.

It is necessary to say 'the specifically characterized phenomenon which is its *object of engagement*' rather than merely saying 'the specifically characterized phenomenon which is its object' because without such specification wrong consciousnesses such as a sense consciousness perceiving white snow mountains as blue or that perceiving the moon as double would have to be considered awarenesses to which an object appears but is not ascertained. This is because to a sense consciousness perceiving the moon as double the specifically characterized phenomenon which is its object clearly appears in that the specifically characterized phenomenon which is its *appearing object* – the single moon – clearly appears to it. However, there is no specifically characterized phenomenon which is its object of engagement, for its object of engagement is a non-existent phenomenon – such as blue snow mountains or a double moon. Thus, the definition is so worded in order to eliminate these non-conceptual wrong consciousnesses from being awarenesses to which the object appears but is not ascertained.

There is also a reason for the definition specifying 'the specifically characterized phenomenon *which is* its object of engagement', rather than just saying 'a specifically characterized phenomenon, its object of engagement'. One can posit as an example of such a mind a direct perceiver apprehending sound at a time the mind is attached to a beautiful form, and one can ask the question, 'Does its object of engagement, a specifically characterized phenomenon, clearly appear?' If the answer given is yes, then one can ask, 'Is "its object of engagement" a specifically characterized phenomenon?' The play in this debate is on the fact that 'its object of engagement' is permanent from the viewpoint of its self reverse (*rang ldog*), and thus one has incurred a verbal fault by leaving out the qualifying phrase 'which is' which serves to eliminate the general usage of the term.

The meaning of the phrase 'is unable to induce ascertainment' in the above definition is that this knower is unable later to induce an ascertaining consciousness (*nishchaya-jñāna, nges shes*) which knows that one saw the object. Ascertaining consciousnesses are necessarily conceptual consciousnesses; one does not use this term in reference to sense consciousnesses.

> When awarenesses to which objects appear but are not ascertained are divided, there are three: sense, mental, and self-knowing direct perceivers which are awarenesses to which an object appears but is not ascertained. [6b.3–4]

If one is attending a dance performance and is engrossed in the music, the sense consciousness which one generates viewing the colours and shapes of the performers would be instances of sense direct perceivers to which the object appears but is not ascertained. One might see the performers but would not ascertain them, due to one's attention being concentrated on the music. On the other hand, one might be particularly attached to the beautiful forms, and then the sounds would appear to and be apprehended by the ear consciousness, but it would be unable subsequently to induce ascertainment of them, to remember them. Another illustration is a time when one is walking along a road while involved in conversation with someone, and has a sense of people passing by but later cannot remember who they were. Sometimes we read and then afterwards think, 'What did I read?' and have no idea. This, too, is appearance of the object without ascertainment.

An illustration of a mental direct perceiver to which the object appears but is not ascertained is, as explained earlier (page 59), a mental direct perceiver apprehending a form, or a sound, or an odour, etc., in the continuum of an ordinary being.

An illustration of a self-knowing direct perceiver to which an object appears but is not ascertained is a self-knower experiencing a mental direct perceiver apprehending a form in the continuum of an ordinary being. A few presentations of 'Awareness and Knowledge' posit as an illustration of this a self-knower in the continuum of a Nihilist (*Ayata, rGyang 'phen pa*) experiencing an inferential prime cognizer. This illustration is posited because Nihilists, although they have inferential prime cognizers, say that they do not, for they assert that the only prime cognizer is a direct perceiver and thus assert that inferential prime cognizers do not exist. Because they do not accept the existence of a consciousness which nonetheless occurs in their mental continuums, it is said that the self-knower experiencing an inferential prime cognizer in the continuum of such a person is a case of an awareness to which the object appears but is not ascertained. However, not all textbooks accept this as an instance of such, for it can be said that the self-knower realizes the inferential prime cognizer, but just does not realize it *as* an inferential prime cognizer.

Another similar illustration, which some textbooks posit as a self-knowing direct perceiver to which an object appears but is not ascertained, is a self-knower in the continuum of a Sāṃkhya or Vaisheṣhika experiencing a blissful consciousness. Proponents of these two systems do not assert that bliss is a consciousness but say that it is matter. In our own system bliss is a type of the mental factor feeling and is a consciousness. There are physical pliancies which are a physical bliss, and since those would be an object of touch and thus matter, the subject which is posited here is 'a blissful *consciousness*', eliminating by the wording any reference to a physical bliss. Because Sāṃkhyas and Vaisheṣhikas do not assert the existence of such a blissful consciousness, the self-knower experiencing a blissful consciousness in the continuum of a Sāṃkhya or Vaisheṣhika would be an awareness to which the object appears but is not ascertained. However, as in the previous example, there is debate on this among the various textbooks, some saying that the self-knower realizes the blissful consciousness but does not realize the bliss as a consciousness.

Thus, among awarenesses to which the object appears but is

not ascertained, there are sense, mental, and self-knowing direct perceivers, but no yogic direct perceivers.

> Yogic direct perceivers which are such do not exist because any yogic direct perceiver must realize its object. This is because it says in Dharmakīrti's *Commentary on (Dignāga's) 'Compendium on Prime Cognition'*, 'From just seeing, the great intelligent ones ascertain all aspects.' [6b.4–7a.1]

There are many different ways of interpreting this statement by Dharmakīrti. According to Jam-yang-shay-ba, whatever appears to a yogic direct perceiver must be ascertained by it, whereas Pan-chen Sö-nam-drak-ba says that such is not necessary. His reason for saying this is that there is in the continuum of a Bodhisattva Superior a yogic direct perceiver realizing that an omniscient consciousness is impermanent. To such a yogic direct perceiver an omniscient consciousness appears; however, the yogic direct perceiver does not realize the omniscient consciousness, for if it were to realize it, it would have to realize it directly, and if this were the case, then an omniscient consciousness would have to be within the sphere of a Bodhisattva Superior's direct perception. However, the abandonments and realizations in the continuum of a Buddha are within the sphere of direct perception only of Buddhas, not sentient beings (*sattva, sems can*), and thus, according to Pan-chen Sö-nam-drak-ba it is incorrect to say that a yogic direct perceiver realizes everything that appears to it.

He explains Dharmakīrti's statement, 'From just seeing, the great intelligent ones ascertain all aspects,' as follows. Although the general referent of 'great intelligent ones' is Bodhisattvas, here it refers to yogic direct perceivers. 'Ascertain all aspects' means that a yogic direct perceiver ascertains whatever is its object of engagement – there is nothing which is the object of engagement of a yogic direct perceiver which that consciousness does not realize, although it may not realize everything that appears to it. Because Jam-yang-shay-ba asserts that a yogic direct perceiver does necessarily realize whatever appears to it, he probably would not be willing to say that an omniscient consciousness appears to a yogic direct perceiver in the continuum of a Bodhisattva Superior realizing the impermanence of an omniscient consciousness.

> An illustration of a sense direct perceiver to which an object appears but is not ascertained is a sense direct perceiver apprehending blue which induces the doubt, 'Did I see blue or not?' An illustration of a mental direct perceiver to which an object appears but is not ascertained is a mental direct perceiver apprehending a form in the continuum of an ordinary being. An illustration of a self-knower to which an object appears but is not ascertained is a self-knower in the continuum of a Nihilist that experiences an inference as a prime cognizer. [7a.1–2]

These are the same as the illustrations explained earlier.

> *Doubting consciousnesses*
> The definition of a doubting consciousness is a knower which by its own power has qualms in two directions. [6b.1]

The reason for saying 'by its own power' is that doubt is a mental factor and this qualification eliminates that the main mind and other mental factors which have similarity with it are doubt. The main mind and other factors accompanying the mental factor of doubt also have qualms with regard to their object, but not by their own power; rather, it is through the force of the doubting consciousness that accompanies them.

The meaning of 'in two directions' is that the mind is thinking, 'Is it this or is it that?' 'Qualms' means it is undecided. Doubt is a 'knower' because it is a consciousness.

In the Ra-dö *Awareness and Knowledge*, the definition given for a doubting consciousness is: 'A knower that has qualms with regard to its own object'.

This seems to me to be more correct because the division of awarenesses and knowers into seven is not in terms of minds and mental factors, but a general one. When doubting consciousnesses are defined as knowers which *by their own power* have qualms in two directions, this means that they are mental factors and anything else is eliminated. However, the term 'doubting consciousness' in general includes both minds and mental factors, and thus I feel it is better to use a definition which fits this general usage, leaving off 'by its own power'.

Among the six root afflictions, there is one called doubt. That doubt is necessarily a mental factor and is necessarily afflicted. However, doubt in general is not necessarily either a mental factor or afflicted. It can be posited as of three types: virtuous, non-virtuous, and neutral. A virtuous doubting consciousness would be one that wonders whether or not the effects of actions exist and thinks that probably they do, or one that wonders whether or not former and later lives exist and thinks that probably they do. There definitely is virtuous doubt, for it is said that to develop even doubt with respect to emptiness, thinking that phenomena probably are empty of inherent existence, tears cyclic existence asunder. If this were not virtuous, it would be quite strange that it could tear cyclic existence asunder. The opposites of these virtuous doubting consciousnesses are non-virtuous – such as one which wonders whether or not the effects of actions exist and thinks that they probably do not, or wonders whether or not liberation exists and thinks that it probably does not, or wonders whether or not the path to liberation exists and thinks that it probably does not. The doubt included among the six root afflictions is necessarily non-virtuous.

There are many examples of neutral doubt, for instance, wondering as you are going somewhere whether the person you are going to see will be there or not, or wondering when you wake up in the morning whether it will be sunny or not, or wondering when you make food whether it will be good or not, or wondering whether you put enough sugar in the tea.

Since there are these general uses of the term doubt, it is not good to say that a doubting consciousness within the sevenfold division of awarenesses and knowers must be either a mind or a mental factor. This is true of all seven within this division; they should not be posited from the viewpoint of being minds or mental factors but in general. However, when defining the doubt which is included within the six root afflictions, one should include the qualification 'by its own power'. Its definition is: 'an affliction which by its own power has qualms in two directions.'

Thus the main mind which accompanies afflicted doubt would not be a case of the doubt which is one of the root afflictions although it is a doubting consciousness. The reason for this is that whatever is one of the six root afflictions must be a mental factor and thus included within the fifty-one mental factors.

> When doubting consciousnesses are divided, there are three: tending toward the fact, not tending toward the fact, and both equally. An illustration of doubt tending toward the fact is a two-pointed mind thinking, 'Sound is probably impermanent'. [6b.1–2]

The first is called tending toward the fact because it is close to being factually concordant – it is about to become concordant with the fact. If one does not meet with bad circumstances, it will become factually concordant, but if one meets with bad circumstances such as a wrong teacher or bad friends it will not. For instance, you could read a wrong book and be led to think, 'This is wrong, sound is not impermanent after all,' and would thus generate a mind which was not factually concordant. However, most cases of doubt tending toward the fact do become factually concordant minds.

> An illustration of doubt not tending to the fact is a two-pointed mind thinking, 'Sound is probably permanent.' [6b.2]

Unless very fortunate conditions are met with, this kind of doubt mostly turns into a mind which does not accord with the fact – a wrong consciousness. However, if one meets with a good teacher or reads a good book, it is still possible to generate a factually concordant mind.

> An illustration of equal doubt is a hesitating consciousness which wonders whether sound is permanent or impermanent. [6b.2–3]

Depending on the circumstances ones meets with, this type of doubt can turn into either a factually concordant or discordant mind.

Doubting consciousnesses are among the worst types of mind. If one is travelling along a road constantly wondering, 'Is this the right road or not,' it is difficult to arrive at one's destination. Similarly, if one is on a path of liberation and constantly wonders, 'Is this a path of liberation or not?' 'Will this help or not?' 'Can I attain liberation or not?' it is difficult to make any progress in one's meditation.

Wrong consciousnesses

The definition of a wrong consciousness is a knower which is mistaken with regard to its object of operation. [7a.2]

It is necessary that this definition says 'object of engagement' and not just 'object', for all thought consciousnesses are mistaken with regard to their own objects in that they are all mistaken with regard to their appearing objects since images of their objects seem to be the actual things. Thus, if one posited as the definition of a wrong consciousness: 'a knower which is mistaken with regard to its own object', one would have to say that inferential prime cognizers such as those realizing impermanence and selflessness are wrong consciousnesses, and this is not suitable. These consciousnesses are not mistaken with regard to their objects of engagement – impermanence and selflessness – and thus are not wrong consciousnesses.

Another definition sometimes posited is: 'a knower which is mistaken with regard to its determined object'.

This too is incorrect because determined objects are not posited for non-conceptual consciousnesses, and thus such awarenesses as sense consciousnesses perceiving blue snow mountains, which are in fact wrong consciousnesses, could not fulfil the definition.

Thus, the definition given by Ge-shay Jam-bel-sam-pel is that found in most textbooks.

When wrong consciousnesses are divided, there are two: conceptual and non-conceptual. Illustrations of conceptual wrong consciousnesses are a thought consciousness apprehending the horns of a rabbit and a consciousness apprehending a self of persons. [7a.2–3]

One could also posit a thought apprehending blue snow mountains or a thought apprehending a white conch as yellow.

There are two types of non-conceptual wrong consciousnesses: sense and mental. Wrong sense consciousnesses are, for example, a sense consciousness seeing two moons or a sense consciousness to which snow mountains appear blue. A wrong mental consciousness is, for example, a dream consciousness to which blue clearly appears. [7a.3–4]

There is discussion as to whether dream consciousnesses are conceptual or non-conceptual. People tend to think they are conceptual; however, Tsong-ka-pa does appear to say at one point in his *Ocean of Reasoning, Explanation of (Nāgārjuna's) 'Treatise on the Middle Way'* that there are non-conceptual ones as well.

This concludes the division of awarenesses and knowers into seven. Why is such a division made? Some say it is to eliminate wrong ideas, such as the Nihilist assertion that direct perception is the only prime cognizer or the Vaisheṣhika assertion that there are no subsequent cognizers. I feel that it is mainly made for the sake of identifying the various types of minds.

5. *Division of Awareness and Knowledge into Three*

The division of awareness and knowledge into three consists of (1) conceptual consciousnesses that take a meaning generality as their apprehended object, (2) non-conceptual non-mistaken consciousnesses that take a specifically characterized phenomenon as their apprehended object, and (3) non-conceptual mistaken consciousnesses that take a clearly appearing non-existent as their apprehended object.

Conceptual consciousness that takes a meaning generality as its apprehended object and conceptual consciousness are synonymous. [7a.4–7b.2]

If conceptual consciousnesses are divided, there are two: those which accord with the fact and those discordant with the fact. We make the general statement that with regard to any thing that exists, the conceptual consciousness apprehending it is necessarily one which accords with the fact. In contrast to this, thought consciousnesses which do not accord with the fact are those apprehending non-existent phenomena such as the horns of a rabbit, the permanence of sound, a self of persons, etc. They are wrong consciousnesses.

Non-conceptual non-mistaken consciousness that takes a specifically characterized phenomenon as its apprehended object and direct perceiver are synonymous. [7b.2]

The same fourfold division that is made for direct perceivers – sense, mental, self-knowing, and yogic – can be made for non-conceptual non-mistaken consciousnesses that take a specifically characterized phenomenon as their apprehended object.

> Non-conceptual mistaken consciousness that takes a clearly appearing non-existent as its apprehended object and non-conceptual wrong consciousness are synonymous. [7b.2]

Among wrong consciousnesses there are those which are mistaken with respect to shape, colour, activity, entity, number, time, and size. A sense consciousness to which a firebrand appears to be a wheel is mistaken with respect to shape. That to which a white conch appears as yellow or a white snow mountain appears as blue is mistaken with respect to colour. That to which trees appear to be moving is mistaken with respect to activity; that to which the one moon appears double is mistaken with respect to number; and a sense consciousness to which falling hairs appear is mistaken with respect to entity. If one dreams at night that it is daytime and the sun is shining, the mind is mistaken with respect to time. If one is on a vast plain and looks off into the distance, large things will appear small and small ones large; this is error with respect to size.

Any consciousness that takes a clear appearance of a non-existent as its apprehended object is a mistaken consciousness. However, not everyone agrees that all such are wrong consciousnesses, stating as exceptions such minds as the meditative stabilization on ugliness in which one sees the whole area as unpleasant or the meditative stabilization on the earth-totality or the water-totality in which one sees nothing but earth or water. It is said that if one meditates strongly, even on something that is not true, through the power of increasing familiarity one can come to have a non-conceptual clear appearance of it. These meditative stabilizations just cited have such a clear appearance of a non-existent. However, according to some scholars they are not wrong consciousnesses.

That they have a clear appearance of a non-existent is stated in the root text of Dharmakīrti's *Commentary on (Dignāga's)*

'*Compendium on Prime Cognition*'. Also, later on in the same text Dharmakīrti says 'the remainder are polluted', with the referent of 'remainder' being these same meditative stabilizations, and 'polluted' meaning that they are polluted by causes of error as the line is explained by Kay-drup Rin-bo-chay in his *Great Commentary*. Moreover, later in Kay-drup's commentary on this, he asks, 'Are these meditative stabilizations on only earth, water, and so forth not yogic direct perceivers?' and answers his own question, 'No, they are not'. They are awarenesses which through the force of meditation have a clear appearance of the aspect of the object; they are non-conceptual consciousnesses. But, because they are mistaken, they are not yogic direct perceivers.

There is also a sūtra which seems to indicate that such meditative stabilizations are mistaken. Thus, in dependence on such sources, it would seem that meditative stabilizations on ugliness, the earth-totality, water-totality and so forth have to be considered non-conceptual mistaken consciousnesses. At this time of teaching about 'Prime Cognition' we are mainly speaking of the Sautrāntika system, according to which non-conceptual mistaken consciousness and non-conceptual wrong consciousness are synonymous. Thus, if one is willing to say that these meditative stabilizations are mistaken, one has also to say they are wrong.

However, Chandrakīrti says in his *Supplement to the Middle Way* (*Madhyamakāvatāra*) that these meditative stabilizations on ugliness, the earth-totality, and so forth are cases of taking an unreality to mind [for a specific purpose such as suppressing desire]. Thus, when teaching about Mādhyamika, teachers usually say that these meditative stabilizations are not wrong consciousnesses but just unreal mental applications.

If something is a non-conceptual wrong consciousness, then it is a superimposing one; all such are objects to be abandoned. If one accepts this, one has to say that a Buddha, who has abandoned all objects of abandonment, could not have in his continuum these types of meditation on ugliness, water-totality, earth-totality, and so forth, whereas, since he is the best of meditators, he obviously does. Because of this problem, many people take these statements from sūtra, Dharmakīrti, and Kay-drup as requiring interpretation rather than literally. They say that these meditative stabilizations do have clear appearance but are neither wrong nor mistaken because yogis engage in these meditations intentionally for a specific purpose and consequently they are not affected by any cause of error, either superficial or deep. Therefore, they conclude that not all consciousnesses that take as their apprehended object a clear appearance of a non-existent are mistaken.

Others avoid the problem of having to say that a Buddha could not have such meditative stabilizations in a different way. They accept the explicit statements of sūtra, Dharmakīrti, and Kay-drup Rin-bo-chay that these are mistaken consciousnesses and say as well that they are wrong. However, they assert that this does not mean they have to be superimposing consciousnesses. According to them, any wrong or mistaken consciousness affected by either a superficial or deep cause of error must be a superimposing consciousness, but these meditative stabilizations are not such. They are cultivated without being affected by causes of error and for a purpose. Therefore, they are not superimposing consciousnesses and not objects of abandonment.

In a similar way, there are three types of Mahāyāna mind-generation (*chittotpāda, sems bskyed*): that like a boatman, shepherd, and a king. That like a boatman is a mind-generation in which one thinks that oneself and all other sentient beings should attain Buddhahood together. That like a shepherd is the mind-generation of one who thinks to establish all other sentient beings in Buddhahood first and then attain it himself. One might attempt to debate about these types of mind-generation, saying that they would never actually occur, but Tsong-ka-pa says in his *Golden Rosary of Good Explanation* that it is not a suitable topic for debate, because Bodhisattvas have many impossible wishes. For his own purposes, in order to make his thought more vast, a Bodhisattva does have such wishes although there are actually no cases of everyone becoming enlightened together, or of everyone else going first and oneself attaining Buddahood afterwards.

My own feeling is that there are many cases of mind-training in which one is taking to mind something that does not actually occur and by that means greatly increasing one's force of mind. This is the case in such meditations as those on ugliness, water-totality, and earth-totality. Even though these are unreal mental applications, I do not feel that they are superimpositions or objects to be abandoned. On the contrary, they are to be cultivated.

6. Prime Cognizers

> The division of awareness and knowledge into two [can be done in many ways]: prime cognizers and non-prime consciousnesses; conceptual and non-conceptual consciousnesses; mistaken and non-mistaken consciousnesses; mental and sense consciousnesses; awarenesses which are eliminative engagers and collective engagers; and minds and mental factors. [7b.3–4]

Dividing awarenesses and knowers in these various ways into seven, three, and two is for the sake of understanding well the presentation of mind. One will recognize these different types of awarenesses and understand how they are contained within each other.

> *Prime cognizers and non-prime consciousnesses*
> The definition of a prime cognizer is a new incontrovertible knower. [7b.4]

This definition is used by the Sautrāntikas, Chittamātrins, and Svātantrikas. The Sanskrit word for prime cognizer is *pramāṇa*. According to these systems, *pra* (prime) means first, and *māna* means comprehend; thus the meaning of *pramāṇa* is to comprehend an object initially, or newly. However, in Prāsaṅgika, *pra* is taken to mean main and *māṇa* comprehend; thus *pramāṇa* means that which is incontrovertible with regard to its main object. Those systems which take *pramāṇa* as meaning to comprehend an object newly define a prime cognizer as a 'new incontrovertible knower'. The term 'new' eliminates subsequent cognizers from being prime cognizers and is specifically stated in order to contrast their assertion to the Prāsaṅgika view that subsequent cognizers are prime.

The term 'incontrovertible' eliminates awarenesses to which an object appears but is not ascertained, correctly assuming, doubting, and wrong consciousnesses. 'Knower' eliminates that the sense powers are prime cognizers as the Vaibhāṣhikas assert. It also eliminates, as some non-Buddhists assert, that the person or the sounds of the Vedas are prime cognizers. Within Buddhism, there is a threefold terminological division of *pramāṇa* into persons such as Buddha, scriptures such as the teaching of the four noble truths, and minds – direct perceivers and inferential cognizers; the term 'knower' eliminates that the first two are actual prime cognizers. There are valid persons and valid scriptures, but they are not prime cognizers, only called that.

What is the meaning of the *new* realization that is mentioned in the definition of a prime cognizer? It is not that this is a mind newly realizing something that was not realized by preceding moments of consciousness of similar type – not, for instance, an eye consciousness realizing something that was not realized by preceding moments of eye consciousness. Such would entail the absurdity that with regard to forms, sounds, odours, tastes, and tangible objects, after one prime cognizer realizing them had been generated, there could never again be generated another.

New realization also cannot be understood as realization of a new object because, for instance, with regard to a sense direct perceiver apprehending a form, the second moment of that consciousness, which is not a prime but a subsequent cognizer, newly realizes the form since the object is new each moment. Thus one would have to say that all moments of the continuum of an eye consciousness apprehending a form were prime cognizers in that each is realizing a 'new' moment of the object. To assert such would contradict the master Dharmottara's statement that the first moments of direct perceivers and inferential cognizers are prime cognizers and later moments subsequent ones. Thus new realization cannot refer to newness of the object.

The correct meaning is that a prime cognizer newly realizes its object *by its own power* without doing so through the force of a former prime cognizer which induces it. Thus one can make the distinction that the second moment of an omniscient consciousness is a prime cognizer because it newly realizes its object through its own power, whereas the second moment of a sense direct perceiver is a subsequent cognizer because, although having as its object a phenomenon which is being newly realized, it engages that object merely through the force of a former prime cognizer – its own first moment.

One can understand what it means for something to operate under its own power through the example of a Buddha, for when a Buddha teaches doctrine, it is through his own power. However, when others like ourselves teach, it is through the power of others – from Buddha through to one's own lama. For example, a Buddha first sets forth a doctrine, then later lamas give commentary on it; we come to understand it to some degree, based on our understanding develop belief in it, and then explain it to others.

> When prime cognizers are divided, there are two: direct and inferential. This enumeration of prime cognizers as two is definite, for more than these would be unnecessary and less would not include them all. However, this definite enumeration eliminates wrong conceptions, not any third possibility, for whatever is a prime cognizer is not necessarily one of those two. This is because it is difficult to posit prime cognizer in general as either of those two. [7b.4–8a.2]

Dharmakīrti, in his *Commentary on (Dignāga's) 'Compendium on Prime Cognition'*, proves extensively that there are only two prime cognizers by way of showing that more than two are unnecessary and less than two would not include them all. However, if someone asks whether whatever is a prime cognizer is necessarily one of these two, one must answer no, because one can posit certain general subjects which are neither, such as just prime cognizer itself or a prime cognizer in a specific person's mental continuum, or a prime cognizer of today, or yesterday, or tomorrow.

There are two opinions as to whether the definite enumeration of prime cognizers as two eliminates any third possibility or not. The author of this text has taken the position that it does not because of these exceptions which are neither, such as the general prime cognizer. Others say that this enumeration does eliminate any third possibility because when you search for a final particular instance of a prime cognizer, one can posit nothing other than a direct or an inferential one. Both views provide a source for thought. Regardless of this difference, both groups assert that the number of prime cognizers is definite as two, and prove it based on the fact that there is a twofold division of objects of comprehension into specifically and generally characterized phenomena.

> The enumeration of prime cognizers as two is definite because the lord of reasoning [Dharmakīrti] said [in the third chapter of his *Commentary on (Dignāga's) 'Compendium on Prime Cognition'*], 'Because objects of comprehension are two, prime cognizers are two.' [8a.1–3]

Whatever is an object of comprehension by a prime cognizer is necessarily either a specifically or a generally characterized phenomenon. Specifically characterized phenomena are taken as the apprehended objects of direct prime cognizers and generally characterized ones as those of inferential prime cognizers. Because all objects of comprehension are in this sense taken as the objects of just these two prime cognizers, the number of prime cognizers is definitely two.

The main reason for this assertion as to number is not to eliminate any third possibility – for one can argue well both sides of this position – but rather to clear away wrong ideas:

> He [Dharmakīrti] says this in order to refute the many wrong ideas which had arisen with regard to that enumeration – from the Nihilists' positing one, direct perception, to the Dza-ri-ga-bas' (Tsa-ri-ka-pa) positing eleven. Refuting those well from many

> viewpoints of reasoning by the power of the fact, Dharmakīrti establishes a definite enumeration of prime cognizers as those two. [8a.2–4]

The wrong view of the Nihilists is that except for direct perception there is no other prime cognizer. They say that what one sees is what exists and what one does not see does not exist. Hidden phenomena do not exist and thus there can be no prime cognizer that realizes them. Therefore, they say that inference does not exist and the only prime cognizer is direct perception.

The Sāṃkhyas assert three prime cognizers: direct, inferential, and arisen from sound, the third being a consciousness that apprehends a hidden phenomenon in dependence on sound – for instance, when you tell someone that something is so and in dependence on your speech the person realizes it. They say that this is a mental application with regard to a hidden phenomenon and thus is not a direct prime cognizer. It also is not an inferential one because it is not generated in dependence on a correct reason; hence they posit it as a third type of prime cognizer. In our system, we call such a correctly assuming consciousness because it is induced by a mere term and does not realize its object.

The Naiyāyikas assert four prime cognizers: the former three plus one which apprehends its object by means of an example. For instance, from seeing a cow without a dewlap, one can understand that a sentient being similar to this is a bullock. One is not actually seeing the bullock and thus it is a hidden phenomenon which one apprehends through an example.

The Jainas assert six prime cognizers: the previous four plus a contextual one and one that realizes objects other than those realized by the first five. An example of a contextual prime cognizer is one realizing that the live Devadatta is outside because he is not inside.

The Dza-ri-ga-bas, who are probably a subdivision of the Vaisheṣhikas, assert eleven prime cognizers: these six plus reasoning, non-observation, renown, existence, and one that is something like doubt.

Thus, there are many wrong assertions as to the number of prime cognizers and in order to refute them, Dharmakīrti set forth the proof, 'Because objects of comprehension are two, prime cognizers are two.' At this point one might ask, 'Is there not a Buddhist system, Prāsaṅgika, which asserts four prime cognizers: direct, inferential, scriptural, and by way of an example?' However, these four do not exceed the definite enumeration as two, for a scriptural prime cognizer is the same as an inferential one by way of belief and that by way of an example can be included within inferential prime cognizers by the power of the fact. Thus, the latter two are not separate from inferential prime cognizers, and hence among Buddhist tenet systems there is none which does not say that the number of prime cognizers is definite as two.

Within the twofold division of prime cognizers into direct and inferential, there are subdivisions which have already been discussed. There are four types of direct prime cognizers – sense, mental, self-knowing, and yogic – and three types of inferential cognizers – those through belief, by the power of the fact, and through renown.

There is another way that prime cognizers can be divided: into those which induce ascertainment by themselves (*svataḥ prāmāṇya, rang las nges kyi tshad ma*) and those when ascertainment is induced by another (*parataḥ prāmāṇya, gzhan las nges kyi tshad ma*). For instance, one might look off in the distance and see something like the colour of fire; however, because it is far away, one cannot ascertain if it actually is the colour of fire – cannot realize it. Thus what is the eye consciousness – the sense direct perceiver – apprehending? It is perceiving merely a reddish colour. Only in dependence on a subsequent prime cognizer when one approaches nearer can ascertainment as to the colour of fire be induced. Thus the original sense direct perceiver is not a prime cognizer which induces ascertainment by itself, but rather one when ascertainment is induced by another.

One can posit as its object of comprehension the reddish colour; however, the *final nature* of its object of comprehension is the colour of fire. The colour red is only the measure of the appearance of the object and not the measure of its actual status. Thus, a sense direct perceiver apprehending it is not perceiving the final nature of the object of comprehension – it is not getting at a final object with respect to which superimpositions have been removed. If the colour of the fire were not with the object being perceived – the reddish colour – the sense direct perceiver would not arise, but the consciousness apprehending the reddish colour is unable to induce ascertainment with respect to the colour of fire itself, is unable to ascertain the connection between the reddish colour and the colour of fire which is its final nature. In fact, the colour of fire is the cause of the sense direct perceiver apprehending the reddish colour, for if that colour of fire did not exist, a sense direct perceiver apprehending a reddish colour could not be produced. However this cannot be ascertained by the mind apprehending the reddish colour; ascertainment must be induced in dependence on another prime cognizer which must arise subsequent to it, and for this reason the sense direct perceiver apprehending the reddish colour is called a prime cognizer when ascertainment is induced by another. In the phrase 'when ascertainment is induced by another', 'another' refers to a later prime cognizer, and 'ascertainment' refers to ascertainment of the colour of fire.

To understand prime cognizers which induce ascertainment by themselves, consider a sense direct perceiver in the continuum of a son apprehending his father's form. This sense direct perceiver takes as its object the father's form, and the final nature of that object is the father's form. In the Sautrāntika system, the form of the father has to exist as the mode of being, or the status, of the object, and if it did not so exist, right with the object, the sense direct perceiver in the continuum of the son apprehending it could not arise. The son's eye consciousness is itself able to induce ascertainment with respect to this connection – the relationship between the non-arising of itself if the final nature of the father's form did not exist right with the object – without having to depend on another prime cognizer. Thus it is called a prime cognizer which induces ascertainment by itself.

Thus, the text says:

> In another way prime cognizers are also twofold: those which induce ascertainment by themselves and those when ascertainment is induced by another. The definition of a prime cognizer that induces ascertainment by itself is a new incontrovertible knower which is able to induce through its own power ascertainment that it itself would not arise if the final nature of its object of comprehension did not abide in the object. The definition of a prime cognizer when ascertainment is induced by another is a new incontrovertible knower that is unable to induce such [ascertainment] but must depend on another later conventional prime cognizer. [8a.4–8b.2]

Ge-shay Jam-bel-sam-pel's definition of a prime cognizer when ascertainment is induced by another is abbreviated. In full form it is: 'a new incontrovertible knower which is unable to induce ascertainment that it itself would not arise if the final nature of its object of comprehension did not abide in the object but must depend on another later conventional prime cognizer'.

Here the later *conventional* prime cognizer does not, as in Mādhyamika, refer to prime cognizers analysing the conventional as opposed to the ultimate, but is a prime cognizer that knows verbal conventions.

> When prime cognizers which induce ascertainment by themselves are divided, there are five: sense direct prime cognizers having a familiar object, sense direct prime cognizers to which the ability to perform a function appears, self-knowing direct prime cognizers, yogic direct prime cognizers, and inferential prime cognizers.
>
> An illustration of a sense direct prime cognizer having a familiar object is a sense direct perceiver in the continuum of a son apprehending his father's form. [8b.2–3]

One could also posit a sense direct perceiver in the continuum of a girl apprehending her own watch. This is a sense consciousness apprehending any object with which one has some familiarity; it is sufficient to induce ascertainment of the object.

> An illustration of a sense direct prime cognizer to which the ability to perform a function appears is a sense direct perceiver which, apprehending fire, comprehends that fire is able to perform the function of cooking and burning. [8b.3]

One could also posit a sense direct perceiver which, apprehending water, comprehends – without any further thought – that water is able to perform the function of wetting and moistening, or one that apprehends a land area as able to act as a basis, or support. In all these examples it is the sense direct perceiver itself which comprehends that its object is able to perform a function – the eye consciousness *sees* that fire can cook and burn, that water can wet and moisten, and so forth.

> An illustration of a self-knowing direct prime cognizer is a self-knowing direct perceiver that experiences a prime cognizer. An illustration of a yogic direct prime cognizer is a wisdom consciousness directly realizing the selflessness of the person. [8b.4]

A wisdom consciousness directly realizing the selflessness of the person is called direct realization (*mngon sum du rtogs pa*) because it is realizing that selflessness by the power of experience and not by way of a meaning generality. However, it is, in the Sautrāntika system, an implicit realization rather than an explicit one because the aspect of the object – the selflessness of the person – does not actually appear to it since it is a permanent phenomenon and thus not an appearing object of direct perception. Some scholars make a distinction between 'directly realize' (*mngon sum du rtogs pa*) and 'realize by means of a direct perceiver' (*mngon sum gyis rtogs pa*), saying that a yogic direct perceiver realizing the selflessness of the person realizes that selflessness by means of a direct perceiver but not directly.

> An illustration of an inferential prime cognizer is an inferential cognizer realizing sound to be impermanent.

> Such [a fivefold division of prime cognizers able to induce ascertainment by themselves] is the thought of Sa-gya Pandita's *Treasury of Reasoning*, which says, 'The two knowers of objects, the two self-knowers, and inference ascertain by themselves.' [8b.4–9a.1]

'The two knowers of objects' refers to a sense direct prime cognizer having a familiar object and one to which the ability to perform a function appears. 'Two self-knowers' refers to self-knowing and yogic direct prime cognizers. Yogic direct perceivers are often called individual self-knowers (*so sor rang rig*) to emphasize the need for a yogi's own individual realization and thus here are included within self-knowers.

> When prime cognizers when ascertainment is induced by another are terminologically divided, there are three: those when ascertainment of the appearance is induced by itself but ascertainment of the truth is induced by another; when ascertainment of the general is induced by itself, but ascertainment of the particular is induced by another; and when ascertainment of even the mere appearance is induced by another.
>
> Illustrations are as follows: A prime cognizer when ascertainment of the appearance is induced by itself but ascertainment of the truth is induced by another is, for example, a sense direct perceiver apprehending in the distance a reddish colour which is in fact the colour of fire and with respect to which a conceptual consciousness has doubt, wondering, 'Is that the colour of fire or not?' [9a.1–3]

In this example, the appearance with respect to which ascertainment is induced by the sense direct perceiver itself is the reddish colour. The truth with respect to which ascertainment is induced by another is that in fact the reddish appearance is the colour of fire. A later prime cognizer must induce the ascertainment of this.

At this point the various textbooks do not agree; specifically, Jam-yang-shay-ba and Jay-dzun Chö-gi-gyel-tsen differ from Pan-chen Sö-nam-drak-ba. With regard to the above example of fire, the point of discussion is the relationship of the sense direct perceiver to the reddish colour it is apprehending.

Pan-chen Sö-nam-drak-ba says that it is a prime cognizer with respect to the reddish colour, but not one which induces ascertainment by itself with respect to it, whereas Jay-dzun-ba and Jam-yang-shay-ba say that the sense direct perceiver in this example is not even a prime cognizer with respect to the reddish colour, citing as their reason the fact that it is not a prime cognizer which induces ascertainment by itself with respect to the reddish colour.

Jay-dzun-ba and Jam-yang-shay-ba further assert that reddish colour is not the object of comprehension of that sense direct perceiver. However, Pan-chen Sö-nam-drak-ba says that it is the object of comprehension within making the distinction that it is not the final nature of the object of comprehension. Thus in the definitions of prime cognizers when ascertainment is induced by itself and by another as posited by Pan-chen Sö-nam-drak-ba and used by the author of this text, there is included the phrase, 'if the *final nature* of its object of comprehension did not abide in the object'. This does not appear in the definitions given by Jay-dzun-ba and Jam-yang-shay-ba. Thus for Pan-chen the sense direct perceiver in this example realizes its object of comprehension, but not the final nature of that object; however, since the others do not accept even that, they find no need to mention 'final nature' in their definitions.

Pan-chen Sö-nam-drak-ba's reason for positing the reddish colour as the object of comprehension although not the final nature of such is that he asserts it to be the object of comprehension of the measure of appearance, though not of its actual status. He would say that in an example of a prime cognizer which induces ascertainment by itself, such as a sense direct perceiver in the continuum of a son apprehending his father's form, the father's form is both the object of comprehension and the final nature of the object of comprehension and thus is both the object of comprehension of the measure of appearance and that of the measure of its actual status.

A prime cognizer when ascertainment of the general is induced by itself but of the particular by another is, for example, a sense

> direct perceiver apprehending in the distance a tree which is in fact an Ashoka tree[42] and with respect to which a conceptual consciousness has doubt, wondering, 'Is that an Ashoka tree or not?' [9a.3]

The meaning of this example is basically the same as the previous one. The object is in fact an Ashoka, a particular type of tree; however, that which the sense direct perceiver, due to being far from the object, is apprehending is just the generality, tree. Thus the sense direct perceiver is able to induce ascertainment by itself with respect to the generality, the tree, but unable to do so with respect to the particularity, the fact that it is an Ashoka tree. For this ascertainment, it must depend on a later conventional prime cognizer which is generated upon approaching closer.

> A prime cognizer when ascertainment of even the mere appearance is induced by another is, for example, a sense direct perceiver apprehending blue which induces a doubting consciousness that thinks, 'Did I see blue or not?' [9a.4]

This is not an actual prime cognizer when ascertainment is induced by another but is an awareness to which the object appears but is not ascertained. For a consciousness to be a prime cognizer it must be able to induce ascertainment of its object, but here it only induces doubt as to whether or not the colour blue was seen. Thus, amongst the three types of prime cognizers when ascertainment is induced by another, the first two are actually such consciousnesses whereas the third is only an imputed one, and thus this threefold division is terminological. The third is included because inasmuch as it cannot itself induce ascertainment, a person who has it in his continuum must depend on another prime cognizer in order to do so. Since ascertainment is induced by another, it is designated by the name 'prime cognizer when ascertainment is induced by another' even though it is not a prime cognizer.

There is another threefold division of prime cognizers when ascertainment is induced by another which has its source in Sa-gya Pandita's *Treasury of Reasoning*. Our text says:

When prime cognizers when ascertainment is induced by another are terminologically divided in a different way, there are also three: initial direct perceivers, inattentive minds, and those possessing a cause of error. [The source for this division] is the *Treasury of Reasoning* which says, 'Initial, inattentive minds, and those possessing a cause of error are those when ascertainment is induced by another.'

An illustration of an initial direct perceiver is a direct perceiver apprehending the colour of an utpala in the continuum of someone who has not previously experienced seeing an utpala. [9a.4–9b.2]

An utpala is a flower like a bell held upside down which can be blue, gold, white, or red. The example is an actual prime cognizer when ascertainment is induced by another, for it is a prime cognizer with respect to whatever the colour of the flower is but not with respect to the final nature of the object of comprehension, which is the colour of the utpala.

An inattentive mind is, for example, a sense direct perceiver apprehending a sound in the continuum of someone whose mind is at that time greatly attracted to a beautiful form. [9b.2]

This is a terminological rather than actual division of prime cognizers when ascertainment is induced by another. For, it cannot induce ascertainment with respect to the sound, and thus it is not a prime cognizer with respect to it.

A knower possessing a cause of error is, for example, a direct perceiver apprehending the colour of a mirage with respect to which a superimposing consciousness apprehending the mirage as water has actually been generated. [9b.3]

This also is not an actual prime cognizer when ascertainment is induced by another.

This concludes the explanation of prime cognizers; now non-prime consciousnesses will be discussed.

The definition of a non-prime consciousness is a knower which is not new and incontrovertible. When non-prime consciousnesses are divided, there are the latter five [from the division of aware-

> ness and knowledge into seven]: subsequent cognizers, correctly assuming consciousnesses, doubting consciousnesses, awarenesses to which the object appears but is not ascertained, and wrong consciousnesses. [9b.3–4]

There are four possibilities between non-prime consciousness and direct perceiver and between non-prime consciousness and inferential cognizer. Thus, there are direct perceivers which are prime cognizers, such as the first moment of an eye consciousness apprehending blue, and those that are not prime cognizers, such as the second moment of that eye consciousness. The same is true for inferential cognizers – the first moment of an inference realizing sound to be impermanent is prime; the second is not. However, there are only three possibilities each between non-prime consciousness and subsequent cognizer, non-prime consciousness and correctly assuming consciousness, non-prime consciousness and doubting consciousness, non-prime consciousness and awareness to which the object appears but is not ascertained, as well as non-prime consciousness and wrong consciousness. This is because all five are always non-prime consciousnesses since subsequent cognizers are not new and the other four are never incontrovertible.

7. *Other Twofold Divisions of Awareness and Knowledge*

> *Conceptual and non-conceptual consciousnesses*
> The definition of a conceptual consciousness is a determinative knower that apprehends a sound generality and a meaning generality as suitable to be mixed. [9b.4]

According to Pur-bu-jok, there are consciousnesses that apprehend only sound and only meaning generalities, for example apprehending just the sound generality 'pot' without associating it with its meaning or just the meaning generality of pot without associating it with its name. Thus all conceptual consciousnesses are not necessarily cases of the association of a sound and a meaning generality, and, therefore, the definition just cited says that the two are *suitable* to be mixed.

Jam-yang-shay-ba also says that not all conceptual consciousnesses are cases of the association of a sound and a meaning generality. For example, there is a thought consciousness apprehending a pot in the continuum of an ox; it apprehends only a meaning generality since it does not know the term 'pot'. Also, even in the case of a person who knows the verbal convention involved, his thought consciousness realizing an object is not necessarily a case of apprehending a mixture of sound and meaning generalities, for there are thought consciousnesses arisen from meditation such as those realizing impermanence or selflessness which are not apprehending a sound generality. Within the threefold division of consciousnesses into those arisen from hearing, thinking, and meditating, those arisen from hearing definitely depend upon names, those arisen from thinking sometimes depend on names and sometimes do not, and those arisen from meditation do not depend on a name.

This can be explained through the example of swimming. Someone who cannot swim at all must depend upon a life-preserver; someone who can swim a little sometimes needs one and sometimes does not; and someone who has trained well has no need for a life preserver.

When conceptual consciousnesses are divided from the viewpoint of expression, there are two: those affixing names and meanings. The first is a case of a thought consciousness associating the meaning – the object – and its verbal convention, for example, a conceptual consciousness which thinks with respect to a whitish thing that it sees, 'That is an ox,' or one that thinks with respect to something having branches, leaves, and so forth, 'This is a tree.' Such a mind is associating or connecting (*sbyar*) two things – the name learned as the verbal convention and the object understood when later using this convention.

A thought consciousness affixing the meaning is one which apprehends its object within associating the meaning of a substratum and the meaning of attributes. An illustration is a conceptual consciousness that thinks, 'This person is one who has a stick.' The stick is the basis and the person is the attribute, for if you said, 'Whose stick is this?' the answer would be, 'That person's.'

One can also make a twofold division of conceptual consciousnesses into those that do and do not accord with the fact. Conceptual consciousnesses which accord with the fact can be further divided into three: those that are prime cognizers, subsequent cognizers, and those that are not either of those. A prime cognizer which is a factually concordant thought consciousness would be, for instance, the first moment of an inferential cognizer. All conceptual subsequent cognizers such as, for example, the second moment of an inferential cognizer are subsequent cognizers which are thought consciousnesses that accord with the fact. Those which are neither of the former two would be, for example, correctly assuming consciousnesses, which accord with the fact although they are not awarenesses which realize their objects.

If conceptual consciousnesses that do not accord with the fact are divided, there are two: non-realizing ones (**anadhigata-buddhi, ma rtogs pa'i blo*) and wrong ideas (*mithyā-saṃkalpa, log par rtog pa*). A doubting consciousness is a non-realizing thought consciousness. Superimpositions (*āropa, sgro 'dogs*) or denials (*abhyākhyāna, skur 'debs*) are instances of wrong ideas. A superimposition, or superimposing consciousness, is one which adds on something with respect to its object of engagement, as, for example, a thought apprehending sound as permanent or apprehending the mental and physical aggregates as a substantially existent self. Denial, or a denying consciousness, is one that conceives something less than what the actual object of engagement is, one that cuts off some aspect of the object, as, for example, viewing that actions have no effects or that liberation does not exist.

> Conceptual consciousness and awareness which is an eliminative engager are synonymous. [All] inferential cognizers, correctly assuming consciousnesses, and doubting consciousnesses, as well as some subsequent cognizers and wrong consciousnesses, are posited as illustrations of conceptual consciousnesses. [9b.4–10a.]

The reason the text says 'some subsequent cognizers and wrong consciousnesses' is that these two have both conceptual and non-conceptual types. Here the conceptual ones, that is, conceptual subsequent cognizers and conceptual wrong consciousnesses, are posited as instances of conceptual consciousness.

> The definition of a non-conceptual consciousness is a knower which is free from being a determinative knower that apprehends a sound generality and a meaning generality as suitable to be mixed. Non-conceptual consciousness and awareness which is a collective engager are synonymous. [All] direct perceivers and awarenesses to which the object appears but is not ascertained as

well as a portion of subsequent cognizers and wrong consciousnesses are posited as illustrations of non-conceptual consciousness. [10a.1–2]

Thus among the seven types of awareness and knowledge, direct perceivers and awarenesses to which the object appears but is not ascertained are always non-conceptual. Subsequent cognizers and wrong consciousnesses can be either conceptual or non-conceptual. Inferential cognizers, doubting consciousnesses, and correctly assuming consciousnesses are always conceptual.

Mistaken and non-mistaken consciousnesses

The definition of a mistaken consciousness is a knower that is mistaken with regard to its appearing object. Illustrations are all wrong consciousnesses and all conceptual consciousnesses. [10a.2–3]

Among non-conceptual consciousnesses, there are both mistaken and non-mistaken ones. Non-conceptual wrong consciousnesses are necessarily mistaken; all other non-conceptual consciousnesses are necessarily non-mistaken.

Thus, among the seven types of awarenesses and knowers, mistaken consciousness and direct perceiver are contradictory – there is nothing which is both. Between inferential cognizer and mistaken consciousness there are three possibilities – all inferential cognizers are mistaken but there are mistaken consciousnesses which are not inferential cognizers such as correctly assuming consciousnesses. Between subsequent cognizer and mistaken consciousness there are four possibilities – there are subsequent cognizers which are not mistaken such as the second moment of a direct perceiver, and there are mistaken consciousnesses which are not subsequent cognizers such as the first moment of an inferential cognizer. Between correctly assuming consciousness and mistaken consciousness there are three possibilities – all correctly assuming consciousnesses are mistaken consciousnesses but not vice versa. Awarenesses to which an object appears but is not ascertained and mistaken consciousnesses are contradictory – for awarenesses to which the object appears but is not ascertained are necessarily non-mistaken. Between doubting consciousness and mistaken consciousness there are three possibilities, for all doubting consciousnesses are mistaken. There are also three possibilities between wrong consciousness and mistaken consciousness. Any wrong consciousness is a mistaken one, but there are mistaken consciousnesses which are not wrong, such as an inferential cognizer realizing the impermanence of sound.

> The definition of a non-mistaken consciousness is a knower that is not mistaken with regard to its appearing object. Non-mistaken consciousness and direct perceiver are synonymous. However, this is from the viewpoint of the Sautrāntika system; it is not so in the Vijñaptika [Chittamātra] system which asserts both mistaken and non-mistaken direct perceivers. [10a.3–4]

In the Sautrāntika system, any direct perceiver is necessarily a non-mistaken consciousness. However, the Chittamātrins assert both mistaken and non-mistaken direct perceivers. They posit as examples of non-mistaken ones the exalted wisdoms of meditative equipoise in the continuum of a Superior and the exalted knowers in the continuum of a Buddha. They posit as mistaken direct perceivers all those in the continuums of sentient beings, with the exception of Superiors' exalted wisdoms of meditative equipoise [because to all these consciousnesses there is an appearance of subject and object as different substantial entities]. This accords with a general presentation of Chittamātra – the tainted false aspectarian Chittamātrins would posit this somewhat differently.

> *Mental and sense consciousnesses*
> The definition of a mental consciousness is a knower that is produced in dependence on its own uncommon empowering condition, a mental sense power. [10a.4]

The term 'mental consciousness' includes within it both minds and mental factors. Thus the text says:

> Between mind and mental consciousness there are four possibilities: (1) an eye perceiver, for example, is a mind but not a mental consciousness; [10b.1]

One can posit as examples of this any of the sense perceivers – all are minds but not mental consciousnesses.

> (2) all the mental factors accompanying a mental consciousness are mental consciousnesses, but not minds; (3) a mental perceiver is both a mind and a mental consciousness; and (4) all the mental factors accompanying a sense consciousness are neither minds nor mental consciousnesses.
>
> Similarly, there are four possibilities between thought consciousness apprehending a pot and thought consciousness realizing a pot. [10b.2]

The meaning generality of pot must appear to any thought consciousness apprehending a pot, but need not appear to one realizing a pot.

1 A thought apprehending pot is itself both a thought consciousness apprehending pot and a thought consciousness realizing pot.
2 A thought consciousness apprehending the opposite of non-pot is one realizing pot but not apprehending it. This is because the meaning generality of pot does not appear to such a thought consciousness – the meaning generality of opposite from non-pot appears. However, what that consciousness is realizing is pot.
3 A correctly assuming consciousness apprehending pot is an example of a consciousness apprehending pot but not realizing it, since correctly assuming consciousnesses do not realize their objects.
4 Something which is neither is, for example, a thought consciousness apprehending a pillar.

> Also, there are four possibilities between direct perceiver with regard to a phenomenon and direct prime cognizer with regard to a phenomenon. [10b.2]

1 The first moment of a direct prime cognizer realizing the impermanence of sound is both a direct prime cognizer and a direct perceiver with respect to the impermanence of sound.
2 The first moment of a yogic direct perceiver directly realizing the selflessness of a person is a direct prime cognizer with

respect to the selflessness of a person, but is not a direct perceiver with respect to that selflessness. [This is because in the Sautrāntika system the selflessness of a person, being a permanent phenomenon, cannot appear to direct perception although it can be realized directly.]

3 The second moment of a direct perceiver realizing the impermanence of sound is a direct perceiver with respect to the impermanence of sound but not a direct prime cognizer with respect to it.

4 An inferential cognizer realizing the impermanence of sound is neither a direct prime cognizer nor a direct perceiver with respect to the impermanence of sound.

There are four possibilities between inferential prime cognizer with regard to a phenomenon and conceptual consciousness with regard to a phenomenon. [10b.1]

1 An inferential prime cognizer realizing the impermanence of sound is both an inferential prime cognizer and a conceptual consciousness with respect to the impermanence of sound.

2 An inferential prime cognizer realizing that sound is impermanent is an inferential prime cognizer with respect to sound's emptiness of permanence, but is not a conceptual consciousness with respect to it. This is because in order for something to be a conceptual consciousness with respect to sound's emptiness of permanence, a meaning generality of sound's emptiness of permanence must appear to it, and this is not the case in this instance.

3 An inferential prime cognizer realizing the impermanence of sound is a conceptual consciousness with regard to sound, but not an inferential prime cognizer with respect to sound. It is a subsequent cognizer with respect to sound, which it has already realized.

4 A direct prime cognizer realizing the impermanence of sound is neither an inferential prime cognizer nor a conceptual consciousness with respect to the impermanence of sound.

There is a difference between that which is realized from such and such a sign and that which is realized by such and such a sign. [10b.3]

When an opponent realizes that sound is impermanent due to another's stating the proof, 'The subject, sound, is impermanent because of being a product', he realizes not only that sound is impermanent, but also that sound is empty of permanence as well as that sound is opposite from non-impermanent, and so forth. Of those things that he realizes, only the impermanence of sound is realized by such and such a sign, in this case by the sign of being a product; sound's emptiness of permanence, the opposite of non-impermanence, etc., are realized *from* such and such a sign, that is, from the sign of being a product.

Also there is a difference between realizing an object by means of a direct perceiver and realizing it directly. [10b.3]

For example, a yogic direct perceiver directly realizing the selflessness of a person realizes that selflessness by means of a direct perceiver but not directly (*see* p. 124).

Since one should know these distinctions, cherish this terminology of Pan-chen Sö-nam-drak-ba.

The definition of a sense consciousness is a knower that is produced in dependence on its own uncommon empowering condition, a physical sense power. [10b.4–11a.1]

Mental and sense consciousnesses are differentiated by way of their respective sense powers. For example, the sound which comes from a drum is called a drum's sound, a sound from a conch is called a conch's sound, a sprout from rice is called a rice sprout. Similarly the verbal conventions 'sense and mental consciousness' come from the sense powers – physical and mental. Thus, a sense consciousness is that which arises from its own uncommon empowering condition, a physical sense power, and a mental consciousness is that which arises from its own uncommon empowering condition, a mental one.

When sense consciousnesses are divided, there are five: eye, ear, nose, tongue, and body consciousnesses. [11a.1]

Using the eye consciousness as an example, when that of an owl meets with illumination, it does not see forms. For an owl illumination acts as an unfavourable or contradictory condition for the seeing of forms, whereas darkness acts as a favourable one. For a human, illumination acts as a favourable condition for the eye consciousness' seeing forms whereas darkness is a contradictory one. For cats, tigers, leopards, and so forth neither darkness nor illumination act as contradictory conditions for their eye consciousnesses seeing forms; both are favourable. Similarly, water acts as a contradictory condition for the eye consciousness of a human to see forms, but is favourable for a fish. On the other hand, a dry area acts as a contradictory condition for the eye consciousness of an animal whose habitat is water. For animals such as otters and birds that live near water, both water and dry areas are favourable conditions for seeing. Thus, for different types of eye consciousnesses, there is a difference in favourable and contradictory circumstances.

It is important to understand that eye consciousness (**chakṣhur-jñāna, mig shes*) and eye perceiver (*chakṣhur-vijñāna, mig gi rnam par shes pa*) are different. This is true also with respect to ear, nose, tongue, and body consciousnesses. Whatever is, for example, an eye perceiver is necessarily an eye consciousness but there are instances of the latter which are not the former, since eye perceivers are only main minds, whereas eye consciousnesses include both main minds and mental factors.

The five sense consciousnesses are for the most part produced in dependence on observed object conditions. However, there are – in the different tenet systems – various ways of positing these. In the Sautrāntika system, the observed object condition of an eye consciousness is posited as visible forms – colours and shapes. In Chittamātra, however, it is posited as predispositions that exist with the consciousness which is the immediately preceding condition. In the Vaibhāṣhika system any phenomenon, even permanent ones, can be an observed object condition; whatever a consciousness is apprehending is its observed object condition. The Sautrāntika-Svātantrika-Mādhyamikas agree with the Sautrāntikas, whereas the Yogāchāra-Svātantrika-Mādhyamikas agree with the Chittamātrins. The Prāsaṅgikas assert, as do the Sautrāntikas, that forms, colours, shapes, and so forth are the observed object condition of, for example, an eye consciousness; however, unlike the Sautrāntikas they say that these are only imputedly existent observed object conditions.

Similarly, there are differences between the various tenet systems as to how they posit uncommon empowering conditions. Vaibhāṣhika, Sautrāntika, and Sautrāntika-Svātantrika-Mādhyamika assert as the uncommon empowering condition of an eye consciousness a physical sense power which is clear internal matter. The Chittamātrins, on the other hand, posit a potency or a seed; they say that the uncommon empowering condition is form, but not matter. This assertion is probably shared by the Yogāchāra-Svātantrika-Mādhyamikas. The Prāsaṅgikas do not posit the individual subtle particles of the sense power or the collection of particles itself as the uncommon empowering condition but instead posit that which is merely imputed to these as the sense power.

The individual sense powers of the five sense perceivers act as the *uncommon* empowering condition of the respective consciousness. As the *common* empowering condition, one can posit for each the mental sense power. All tenet systems agree that the mental sense power is an immediately preceding moment of any of the six consciousnesses – an immediately preceding mental application. Prāsaṅgika would add to this that it is merely imputed, but they do not disagree with the basic assertion.

These five sense perceivers and the mental perceiver are all minds (*chitta, sems*), perceivers (*vijñāna, rnam shes*), sentience (*manas, yid*). How does the mind abide in the body? There are many different positions on this. Some say that mind's main place of abiding is the brain, whereas others say that it abides at the heart. Some say that it pervades the entire body; some that it does not abide anywhere but is only generated adventitiously upon the contact of an object and a sense power. They say that if it did abide in the body, it would have to abide throughout it, and this would entail the fault that if one cut off a hand, one would be cutting off the continuum of the body consciousness.

I feel that there is no need to say that the mind abides only in the brain or only in the heart – which does not here refer to just the round orb of the heart but to the inner heart; one can say that it abides in both. We ourselves can experience this, for when one withdraws the mind inside, there is a sense as if one is looking out from behind the eyes; thus it would seem that mind abides in the brain. However, when looking at objects outside, it seems as if you are looking from the heart. Moreover, at a time when you touch something with your hand or your foot, a body consciousness and feeling is generated there. At that time it is as if the mind pervades the entire body.

Secret Mantra, the final uncommon system, posits eight main places within the body where the mind abides. In accordance with that system, one must say that the mind abides in all eight, although the main of those are the heart and the head. A sign that these are the main ones is that if someone comes with a stick to harm us, we are willing to give up consideration of our hands and use them to protect our head. In a fight one takes great care not to let a weapon be inserted in the heart or brain, knowing that one will easily die if struck there. However, mind must also abide throughout the body; not to do so would be unsuitable, for the entire body must be conjoined with a continuum of consciousness. The sign of this is that if you stick a pin anywhere in your body, a feeling of discomfort will immediately be generated.

Mind abides in two ways: manifest and dormant. It does not have to be manifest all the time but can be generated from a dormant state immediately upon meeting with an object. If there were not such a conjunction of the continuum of consciousness in either a manifest or dormant manner, immediate generation could not occur. The body is pervaded by the body sense power, and because of this, immediately upon contacting an object, a body consciousness is generated. If you cut off a hand, you cut off a basis of the mind's abiding and cause a severance of the continuum of the particular mind generated in that particular place. However, this does not mean that the continuum of mind in general is cut or that mind has to cease, since mind in general pervades the entire body.

This way in which minds, mental factors, and so forth are generated does not readily appear to us because we are not used to thinking about it. However, through considering it over and over again, one can come to have some sense of the process. For example, if one goes to a store, one generates many different consciousnesses, both simultaneously and serially. It is helpful to identify and analyse them at that time. We usually watch others to see what they are doing rather than watching our own mind to see what it is doing; instead of watching for our own faults, we watch for faults in others. It is best to reverse this.

> *Eliminative and collective engagers*
> The definition of an awareness which is an eliminative engager is a knower that engages its object by the power of terminology. Awareness which is an eliminative engager and conceptual consciousness are synonyms. [11a.1–2]

Many textbooks posit this definition differently, and one should examine to discover which appears more easily to one's mind. For example, in the *Collected Topics of Prime Cognition* of Jay-dzun-ba, Pur-bu-jok, and Ra-dö, the definition is posited as: 'a knower that engages its objects in a partial manner'.

Jam-yang-shay-ba posits: 'a knower that engages its object by way of its own wish'.

Pan-chen Sö-nam-drak-ba gives the same definition as this text: 'a knower that engages its object by the power of terminology'.

The word 'terminology' refers here to a meaning generality. Thus, the explicit object of expression of the sound expressing pot is pot's meaning generality. The determined object of expression is pot. With regard to saying, 'pot', there is a thought consciousness which is the motivation wishing to say 'pot', and through the explicit appearance of pot's meaning generality to that motivating thought consciousness, one says 'pot'. Similarly when thought engages its object, it does so in association with a meaning generality, and thus awarenesses which are eliminative engagers – that is, thought consciousnesses – are ones which engage their objects by the power of terminology.

> The definition of an awareness which is a collective engager is a knower that engages its object by the power of the thing. Awareness which is a collective engager and non-conceptual consciousness are synonymous. [11a.2]

The mind engages in its object through the power of the thing, which is the object's casting its aspect to the mind apprehending it. Both Jay-dzun-ba and Pur-bu-jok posit a different definition: 'a knower that engages its object in a non-partial manner'.

They further posit a threefold division of eliminative engagers into awarenesses, sounds, and persons which are such and a twofold division of collective engagers into awarenesses and persons which are such.

According to Pan-chen Sö-nam-drak-ba and thus according to this presentation of 'Awareness and Knowledge' one would not posit a person of either eliminative or collective engagement. If one were to posit as a person of eliminative engagement an ordinary person [the instance cited by Pur-bu-jok] there is the fault that such a person has in fact both eliminative and collective engagement; at the time conceptual consciousnesses are manifest in his continuum he is an eliminative engager and when directly perceiving ones are manifest he is a collective engager. Moreover, Pan-chen Sö-nam-drak-ba feels that it is not suitable to posit, as does Pur-bu-jok, a Buddha Superior as an instance of a person of collective engagement because a Buddha Superior does not engage objects by the power of the thing; a Buddha's omniscient consciousness does not have to depend on the object, the thing's casting or not casting its aspect to it, but engages in objects by its own power. Because a Buddha's consciousness engages all phenomena without obstruction, it is not the case that he engages some objects which cast their aspect and does not engage others that do not.

> *Minds and mental factors*
> The definition of a mind is that which has similarity with the mental factors that arise as its accompaniers. The three, mind, sentience, and perceiver are synonymous. The definition of a mental factor is that which has similarity with the mind that has it as an accompanier. [11a.3–4]

The statement that minds and the mental factors accompanying them have similarity refers to the five aspects of similarity. Thus, the text says:

> A mode of having similarity exists because, for example, the two, an eye perceiver and the feeling that accompanies it have:
> 1 the same object of observation and thus are similar with regard to object of engagement
> 2 the same mode of apprehension and thus are similar in aspect
> 3 occur at the same time and thus are similar in time

This means that their times of production, abiding and cessation are the same:

> 4 the same uncommon empowering condition and thus are similar in basis
> 5 only a single substantial entity of feeling arises as the accompanier of a single substantial entity of an eye perceiver and thus they are similar in substantial entity

This means that two different substantial entities of feeling or of any other mental factor would not be generated as the accompaniers of one main mind.

> Thus, an eye perceiver and the feeling that accompanies it are similar in five respects.

> These definitions have been made principally for the sake of understanding. If they were to be made principally to eliminate verbal faults, then wherever the word 'itself' occurs in a definition (*lakṣhaṇa, mtshan nyid*) the words 'something's being' must be affixed to the definiendum (*lakṣhya, mtshon bya*). [11a.4–11b.2]

This means, for example, that rather than saying, 'The definition of mind is that which has similarity with the mental factors that arise as *its* accompaniers', one would have to say, 'The definition of *something's being* a mind is that which has similarity with the mental factors that arise as *its* accompaniers.'

> When mental factors are divided, there are six groups:
> 1 the five omnipresent factors: feeling, discrimination, intention, mental engagement, and contact – so-called because they are present as the accompaniers of all main minds.

The omnipresent mental factors accompany all main minds, be they virtuous, non-virtuous, or neutral:

> 2 the five determining factors: aspiration, belief, mindfulness, stabilization, and wisdom – so-called because they are definite to engage in particular objects.
> 3 the eleven virtuous factors: faith, shame, embarrassment, the three root virtues – non-attachment, non-hatred, and non-ignorance – effort, pliancy, conscientiousness, equanimity, and non-harmfulness. These are virtues from the viewpoint of either their entity, being an antidote, or having similarity [that is, accompanying a virtuous mind or mental factor].

These are the mental factors which accompany virtuous main minds. In the Vaibhāṣhika system, ten virtuous mental factors are posited, and any virtuous mind is accompanied by all ten. Here in the Sautrāntika system, eleven are posited, and they need not all accompany every virtuous mind:

> 4 the six root afflictions: desire, anger, pride, ignorance, doubt, and view.[43] The last three must be specified as afflicted. All six are root afflictions because they principally make the mental continuum afflicted.
> 5 the twenty secondary afflictions: belligerence, resentment,

concealment, spite, jealousy, miserliness, deceit, dissimulation, haughtiness, harmfulness, non-shame, non-embarrassment, lethargy, excitement, non-faith, laziness, non-conscientiousness, forgetfulness, non-introspection, and distraction; they are called close [or secondary] afflictions because they are close to and are produced and increase along with root afflictions.

6 the four changeable factors: sleep, contrition, investigation, and analysis – changeable because they will change into virtuous, non-virtuous, or neutral types due to either motivation or accompanying [other mental factors]. [11b.2–12a.4]

If one's motivation is virtuous, non-virtuous, or neutral these mental factors will be the same. For example, if one goes to sleep within a non-virtuous state of mind, one's sleep at least for a while during that night will be non-virtuous, whereas if a virtuous mind is manifest at the time one goes to sleep, one's sleep will be virtuous.

If the intelligent wish to understand the individual natures of these, their functions, substantial entities, signs, differences, and so forth, they can know these in detail from the *Knowledge* (*Abidharma*) texts.

If there are any faults, I confess them to the wise.
If there be virtue, by the power of clearing away
The obscuration of those with low mind like myself
May the teaching of the Conqueror long abide.

This presentation of awareness and knowledge which is a composite of all the important points [has been written] upon repeated urging by all the earlier and later Lo-sel-ling librarians. [I] did not take as my basis the Ra-dö *Awareness and Knowledge* but have set this forth in accordance with Pan-chen [Sö-nam-drak-ba]'s the *Illumination [of the Thought of (Dharmakīrti's) 'Commentary on (Dignāga's) "Compendium on Prime Cognition"']*. Some definitions which were not clear there and were suitable to change I put together in accordance with either A-gya-yong-dzin's (A-kya-yongs-'dzin) *Summary of Awareness and Knowledge* or the Yong-dzin (Yongs-'dzin) [i.e., Pur-bu-jok's] *Awareness and Knowledge*.

Written by the Lo-sel-ling abbot, ge-shay, and recitation

master Jam-bel-sam-pel of Gyel-rong (rGyal-rong) [regional division] in [that division's] temple. The assembled ge-shays have agreed it is correct.

May all virtues increase.

Glossary

ENGLISH	SANSKRIT	TIBETAN
abode	sthāna	gnas
actions	karma	las
adventitious defilements	ākasmika-mala	glo bur gyi dri ma
analysis	vichāra	dpyod pa
anger	pratigha	khong khro
appearing object	*pratibhāsa-viṣhaya	snang yul
apprehend	grahaṇa	'dzin pa
apprehended	grāhya	bzung ba
apprehended object	grāhya-viṣhaya	bzung yul
apprehender	grāhaka	'dzin pa
arisen from hearing	shrutamayī	thos byung
arisen from meditation	bhāvanāmayī	sgom byung
arisen from thought	chintāmayī	bsam byung
ascertaining consciousness	nishchaya-jñāna	nges shes
ascertainment	nishchaya	nges pa
aspect	ākāra	rnam pa
aspiration	chhanda	'dun pa
awareness	buddhi	blo
awareness to which the object appears but is not ascertained	*aniyata-pratibhāsa	snang la ma nges pa
basis	āshraya	rten
belief	adhimokṣha	mos pa
belligerence	krodha	khro ba
calm abiding	shamatha	zhi gnas

ENGLISH	SANSKRIT	TIBETAN
changeable mental factors	*anyathābhāva-chaitta	sems byung gzhan 'gyur
clairvoyance	abhijñā	mngon shes
clairvoyance of divine ear	divya-shrotra- abhijñā	lha'i rna ba'i mngon shes
clairvoyance of divine eye	divya-chakṣhur-abhijñā	lha'i mig gi mngon shes
clairvoyance of knowing others' minds	para-chitta-jñāna-abhijñā	gzhan sems shes pa'i mngon shes
clairvoyance of magical emanation	ṛddhi-abhijñā	rdsu 'phrul gyi mngon shes
clairvoyance of memory of former lifetimes	purva-nivāsānusmṛti-abhijñā	sngon gyi gnas rjes su dran pa'i mngon shes
clear appearance	sputābha	gsal snang
clear form	rūpa-prasāda	gzugs dang ba
clear light	ābhāsvarā	'od gsal
collective engager	*vidhi-pravṛtti	sgrub 'jug
concealment	mrakṣha	'chab pa
conceptual consciousness/ thought/thought consciousness	kalpanā	rtog pa
conceptual subsequent cognizer	*kalpanā-parichchhinna-jñāna	rtog pa bcad shes
conscientiousness	apramāda	bag yod pa
consciousness	jñāna/vijñāna	shes pa/rnam par shes pa
consequence	prasaṅga	thal 'gyur
contact	sparsha	reg pa
contrition	kaukritya	'gyod pa
correct proof	samyak-sādhana	sgrub byed yang dag
correct reason	samyak-nimitta	rgyu mtshan yang dag
correct reasoning	samyak-nyāya	rigs pa yang dag
correct sign	samyak-liṅga	rtags yang dag
correctly assuming consciousness	*manaḥ parīkṣhā	yid dpyod
counter-pervasion	vyatireka-vyāpti	ldog khyab
deceit	māyā	sgyu
deep causes of error	*mukhya-vibhrama-hetu	phug gi 'khrul rgyu
definiendum	lakṣhya	mtshon bya

ENGLISH	SANSKRIT	TIBETAN
definition	lakṣhana	mtshan nyid
denial	abhyākhyāna	skur 'debs
desire	rāga	'dod chags
determinative knower	*adhyavasāya-saṃvedana	zhen rig
determined object	*adhyavasāya-viṣhaya	zhen yul
determining mental factors	*vishayapratiniyama-chaitta	sems byung yul nges
direct perceiver/direct perception	pratyakṣha	mngon sum
direct prime cognizer	pratyakṣha-pramāṇa	mngon sum tshad ma
direct subsequent cognizer	*pratyakṣha-parichchhinna-jñāna	mngon sum bcad shes
directly realize		mngon sum du rtogs pa
discrimination	samjñā	'du shes
dissimulation	shaṭhya	g.yo
distraction	vikṣhepa	rnam par g.yeng ba
doubt/doubting consciousness	vichikitsā/saṃshaya	the tshom
doubt not tending to the fact		don mi 'gyur gyi the tshom
doubt tending to the fact		don 'gyur gyi the tshom
doubting consciousness/ doubt	saṃshaya/vichikitsā	the tshom
effort	vīrya	brtson 'grus
eliminative engager	*apoha-pravṛtti	sel 'jug
embarrassment	apatrāpya	khrel yod pa
emptiness	shūnyatā	stong pa nyid
equal doubt		cha mnyam pa'i the tshom
equanimity	upekṣhā	btang snyoms
exalted knower of all aspects/omniscient consciousness	sarvākārajñāna	rnam mkhyen/rnam pa thams cad mkhyen pa
exalted wisdom	jñāna	ye shes
exalted wisdom of meditative equipoise	samāhita-jñāna	mnyam bzhag ye shes
excitement	auddhatya	rgod pa
explicitly	vastutaḥ	dngos su
eye consciousness	*chakṣhur-jñāna/ chakṣhur-vijñāna	mig shes/mig gi rnam shes
eye perceiver	chakṣhur-vijñāna	mig gi rnam shes
eye sense power	chakṣhur-indriya	mig dbang

ENGLISH	SANSKRIT	TIBETAN
facsimiles of direct perceivers	pratyakṣha-ābhāsa	mngon sum ltar snang
faith	shraddhā	dad pa
feeling	vedanā	tshor ba
forgetfulness	muṣhitasmṛtitā	brjed nges pa
form	rūpa	gzugs
free from conceptuality	kalpanā-apodha	rtog bral
generally characterized phenomenon	sāmānya-lakṣhaṇa	spyi mtshan
harmfulness	vihiṃsā	rnam par 'tshe ba
haughtiness	mada	rgyags pa
Hearer	Shrāvaka	Nyan thos
hidden phenomenon	parokṣha	lkog gyur
ignorance	avidyā	ma rig pa
immediately preceding condition	samanantara-pratyaya	de ma thag rkyen
impermanent phenomenon	anitya-dharma	mi rtag pa'i chos
implicitly	sāmarthyāt	shugs kyi
incontrovertible	avisaṃvādin	mi slu ba
inference/inferential cognizer	anumāna	rjes dpag
inference by the power of the fact	*vastu-bala-anumāna	dngos stobs rjes dpag
inference for another	parārtha-anumāna	gzhan don rjes dpag
inference for oneself	svārtha-anumāna	rang don rjes dpag
inference through belief	*āpta-anumāna	yid ches rjes dpag
inference through renown	*prasidda-anumāna	grags pa'i rjes dpag
inferential cognizer/ inference	anumāna	rjes dpag
inferential prime cognizer	anumāna-pramāṇa	rjes dpag tshad ma
inferential subsequent cognizer	*anumāna-parichchhinna-jñāna	rjes dpag bcad shes
intention	chetanā	sems pa
intermediate state		bar-do
introspection	saṃprajanya	shes bzhin
investigation	vitarka	rtog pa
jealousy	īrṣhyā	phrag dog

ENGLISH	SANSKRIT	TIBETAN
knower	saṃvedana	rig pa
laziness	kausīdya	le lo
lethargy	styāna	rmugs pa
main mind		gtso sems
manifest phenomenon	abhimukhī	mngon gyur
matter	kanthā	bem po
meaning generality	artha-sāmānya	don spyi
meditative stabilization	samādhi	ting nge 'dzin
mental consciousness	mano-jñāna/mano-vijñāna	yid kyi shes pa/yid kyi rnam shes
mental direct perceiver	mānasa-pratyakṣha	yid kyi mngon sum
mental engagement	manasi-kāra	yid la byed pa
mental factor	chaitta	sems byung
mental perceiver	mano-vijñāna	yid kyi rnam shes
mental sense power	mana-indriya	yid dbang
mind	chitta/manas	sems/yid
mind apprehending the sign	*linga-grahaṇa-chitta	rtags 'dzin sems
mindfulness	smṛti	dran pa
mind-generation	chittotpāda	sems bskyed
miserliness	mātsarya	ser sna
mistaken consciousness	bhrānti-jñāna	'khrul shes
negative/negative phenomenon	pratiṣhedha	dgag pa
Nihilist	Ayata	rGyang 'phen pa
non-affirming negative	prasajya-pratiṣhedha	med dgag
non-attachment	alobha	ma chags pa
non-conceptual	nirvikalpaka	rtog med
non-conscientiousness	pramāda	bag med pa
non-embarrassment	anapatrāpya	khrel med pa
non-faith	āshraddhya	ma dad pa
non-harmfulness	avihiṃsā	rnam par mi 'tshe ba
non-hatred	adveṣha	zhe sdang med pa
non-ignorance	amoha	gti mug med pa
non-introspection	asaṃprajanya	shes bzhin ma yin pa
non-mistaken	abhrānta	ma 'khrul pa
non-prime consciousness	apramāṇa-jñāna	tshad min gyi shes pa
non-realizing awareness	*anadhigata-buddhi	ma rtogs pa'i blo
non-shame	āhrīkya	ngo tsha med pa

ENGLISH	SANSKRIT	TIBETAN
object	viṣhaya	yul
object of comprehension	vineya	gzhal bya
object of engagement	*pravṛtti-viṣhaya	'jug yul
object of observation	ālambana-viṣhaya	dmigs yul
object of the mode of apprehension		'dzin stangs kyi yul
object possessor	viṣhayin	yul can
observed object/object of observation	ālambana-viṣhaya	dmigs yul
observed object condition	ālambana-pratyaya	dmigs rkyen
odour	gandha	dri
omnipresent mental factors	sarvatraga-chaitta	sems byung kun 'gro
omniscient consciousness/exalted knower of all aspects	sarvākārajñāna	rnam mkhyen/rnam pa thams cad mkhyen pa
one causal collection		dngos rgyu tshogs pa gcig
path of accumulation	sambhāra-mārga	tshogs lam
path of meditation	bhāvanā-mārga	sgom lam
path of no more learning	ashaikṣha-mārga	mi slob lam
path of preparation	prayoga-mārga	sbyor lam
path of seeing	darshana-mārga	mthong lam
perceiver	vijñāna	rnam shes
perfections	prajñā-pāramitā	phar-phyin
pervasion/positive pervasion	anvaya-vyāpti	rjes khyab
pliancy	prasrabdhi	shin tu sbyang pa
positive/positive phenomenon	vidhi	sgrub pa
potency/power	shakti	nus pa
predicate	sādhyadharma	bsgrub bya'i chos
pride	māna	nga rgyal
prime cognizer	pramāṇa	tshad ma
prime cognizer when ascertainment is induced by another	ērataḥ prāmāṇya	gzhan las nges kyi tshad ma
prime cognizer which induces ascertainment by itself	svataḥ prāmāṇya	rang las nges kyi tshad ma

ENGLISH	SANSKRIT	TIBETAN
realize	adigam	rtogs
realize by means of a direct perceiver		mngon sum gyi rtogs pa
reason	hetu	gtan tshigs
reasoning	nyāya	rigs pa
resentment	upanāha	'khon 'dzin
root afflictions	mūlaklesha	rtsa nyon
secondary afflictions	upaklesha	nye nyon
self-knower	svasaṃvedana	rang rig
self-knowing direct perceiver	svasaṃvedana-pratyakṣha	rang rig mngon sum
selflessness of persons	pudgala-nairātmya	gang zag gi bdag med
sense consciousness	indriya-jñāna/indriya-vijñāna	dbang shes
sense direct perceiver	indriya-pratyakṣha	dbang po'i mngon sum
sense direct perceiver apprehending a form	*rūpa-grahaṇa-indriya-pratyakṣha	gzugs 'dzin dbang mngon
sense perceiver	indriya-vijñāna	dbang po'i rnam shes
sentience/mind	manas	yid
sentient being	sattva	sems can
shame	hrī	ngo tsha shes pa
sign	liṅga	rtags
similarities	samprayukta	mtshungs par ldan pa
similarity of reverse type		ldog pa rigs gcig
similarity of substantial type		rdzas rigs gcig
sleep	middha	gnyid
slightly hidden phenomena	*kimcid-parokṣha	cung zad lkog gyur
smallest moment		dus mtha' skad cig ma
smallest moment in which an action can be completed		bya rdzogs skad cig ma
Solitary Realizer	Pratyeka-buddha	Rang rgyal
sound	shabda	sgra
sound generality	shabda-sāmānya	sgra spyi
special insight	vipashyanā	lhag mthong
specifically characterized phenomenon	svalakṣhaṇa	rang mtshan
spite	pradāsa	'tshig pa
stabilization	samādhi	ting nge 'dzin

ENGLISH	SANSKRIT	TIBETAN
subsequent cognizer	*parichchhinna-jñāna	bcad shes/dpyad shes
substantial entity	dravya	rdzas
substantially existent self	dravya-sat-ātman	rdzas yod kyi bdag
superficial cause of error	*pratibhāshikī-bhrānti-hetu	phral gyi 'khrul rgyu
superimpositions	āropa	sgro 'dogs
Superior	Ārya	'phags pa
syllogism	prayoga	sbyor ba
tangible object	sprașhțavya	reg bya
taste	rasa	ro
terminological suitability		sgra byung grags pa
that which has the aspect of an apprehender	grāhaka-ākāra	'dzin rnam
that which has the aspect of the apprehended	grāhya-ākāra	bzung rnam
thesis	pratijñā	dam bca'
thought/thought consciousness/ conceptual consciousness	kalpanā	rtog pa
three modes	trirūpa	tshul gsum
time	kāla	dus
uncommon empowering condition	asādhārana-adhipati-pratyaya	thun mong ma yin pa'i bdag rkyen
very hidden phenomenon	*atyarthaparokșha	shin tu lkog gyur
view/afflicted view	dṛșhți	lta ba/lta ba nyon mong can
virtuous mental factors	kushala-chaitta	sems byung dge ba
wisdom (*see also* exalted wisdom)	prajñā	shes rab
wisdom arisen from hearing	shrutāmayī-prajñā	thos byung gi shes rab
wrong consciousness	viparyaya-jñāna	log shes
wrong ideas	mithyā-saṃkalpa	log rtog
yogic direct perceiver	yogi-pratyakșha	rnal 'byor mngon sum

Bibliography

Entries in the Tibetan Tripiṭaka Research Foundation publication of the *Tibetan Tripiṭaka* (Tokyo-Kyoto, 1956) are indicated by the letter 'P' (standing for 'Peking edition'), followed by the entry number and volume number.

Āryadeva ('Phags-pa-lha)
Four Hundred/Treatise of Four Hundred Stanzas
Chatuḥshatakashāstrakārikā
bsTan bcos bzhi brgya pa zhes bya ba'i tshig le'ur byas pa
P5246, vol. 95

Asaṅga (Thogs-med)
Compendium of Knowledge
Abhidharmasamuchchaya
mNgon pa kun btus
P5550, vol. 112

Chandrakīrti (Zla-ba-grags-pa)
Supplement to the Middle Way
Madhyamakāvatāra
dbU ma la 'jug pa
P5261, vol. 98; P5262, vol. 98

Den-dar-hla-ram-ba (bsTan-dar-lha-ram-pa, 1759–?)
Presentation of Specifically and Generally Characterized Phenomena
Rang mtshan spyi mtshan gyi rnam bzhag
Collected gsung 'bum of Bstan-dar Lha-ram[s] of A-lag-sha, vol. 1
New Delhi: Lama Guru Deva, 1971

Dharmakīrti (Chos-kyi-grags-pa)
Seven Treatises on Prime Cognition
Analysis of Relations
Saṃbandhaparīkṣhavṛtti
'Brel pa brtag pa'i rab tu byed pa
P5713, vol. 130
Ascertainment of Prime Cognition
Pramāṇavinishchaya
Tshad ma rnam par nges pa
P5710, vol. 130
Commentary on (Dignāga's) 'Compendium on Prime Cognition'
Pramāṇavarttikakārikā
Tshad ma rnam 'grel gyi tshig le'ur byas pa
P5709, vol. 130
Drop of Reasoning
Nyāyabinduprakaraṇa
Rigs pa'i thigs pa zhes bya ba'i rab tu byed pa
P5711, vol. 130
Drop of Reasons
Hetubindunāmaprakaraṇa
gTan tshigs kyi thigs pa zhes bya ba rab tu byed pa
P5712, vol. 130
Proof of Other Continuums
Saṃtānāntarasiddhināmaprakaraṇa
rGyud gzhan grub pa zhes bya ba'i rab tu byed pa
P5716, vol. 130
Reasoning for Debate
Vādanyāyanāmaprakaraṇa
rTsod pa'i rigs pa zhes bya ba'i rab tu byed pa
P5715, vol. 130
Dharmottara (Chos-mchog)
The Correct/Commentary on (Dharmakīrti's) 'Ascertainment of Prime Cognition'
Pramāṇavinishchayaṭīka
'Thad ldan/Tshad ma rnam par nges pa'i 'grel bshad
P5727, vol. 136
Dignāga (Phyogs-glang)
Compendium on Prime Cognition
Pramāṇasamuchchaya
Tshad ma kun las btus pa

P5700, vol. 130
(For a partial translation of this text see next entry)
Hattori, Masaaki
Dignāga, On Perception, being the Pratyakṣapariccheda of Dignāga's 'Pramāṇasamuccaya' from the Sanskrit Fragments and the Tibetan versions
Cambridge, Massachusetts: Harvard University Press, 1968
Jeffrey Hopkins
'Meditation on Emptiness'
unpublished manuscript
See also entries for Jang-gya and Sopa, Geshe Lhundup and Jeffrey Hopkins
Jam-bel-sam-pel, Ge-shay ('Jam-dpal-bsam-'phel, dGe-bshes, ?–1975)
Presentation of Awareness and Knowledge, Composite of All the Important Points, Opener of the Eye of New Intelligence
Blo rig gi rnam bzhag nyer mkho kun 'dus blo gsar mig 'byed
modern blockprint, n.p., n.d.
Jam-yang-shay-ba ('Jam-dbyangs-bzhad-pa, 1648–1721)
Presentation of Awareness and Knowledge
bLo rig gi rnam bzhag
The Collected Works of 'Jam-dByaṅs-bźad-pa'i-rdo-rje, vol. 15
New Delhi: Ngawang Gelek Demo, 1973
Jang-gya Rol-bay-dor-jay (lCang-skya Rol-pa'i-rdo-rje, 1717–86)
'Prasangika-Madhyamika from *Clear Exposition of the Presentation of Tenets*'
dbU ma thal 'gyur pa *from* Grub pa'i mtha'i rnam par bzhag pa gsal bar bshad pa
translated with commentary by Jeffrey Hopkins
unpublished manuscript
Lodrö, Geshe Gedun
Geschichte der Kloster-Universität Drepung
Wiesbaden: Franz Steiner, 1974
Lo-sang-da-yang (bLo-bzang-rta-dbyangs, 1867–1937)
Investigation of the Limits of Pervasion with Respect to Awareness and Knowledge
bLo rig gi mtha' dpyod
The Collected Works of rJe-btsun bLo-bzaṅ-rta-mgrin, vol. 5
New Delhi: Lama Guru Deva, 1975

McDermott, Charlene
'Direct Sensory Awareness: A Tibetan View and a Medieval Counterpart'
Philosophy East and West, vol. 23 (1973), pp. 343–59

Na-wang-bel-den (Ngag-dbang-dpal-ldan, 1797–?)
Explanation of the Meaning of 'Conventional' and 'Ultimate' in the Four Tenet Systems
Grub mtha' bzhi'i lugs kyi kun rdzob dang don dam pa'i don rnam par bshad pa
New Delhi: Lama Guru Deva, 1972

Pan-chen Sö-nam-drak-ba (Paṇ-chen bSod-nams-grags-pa, 1478–1554)
Illumination of the Thought, Commentary on the Difficult Points of (Dharmakīrti's) 'Commentary on (Dignāga's) "Compendium on Prime Cognition"'
Tshad ma rnam 'grel gyi dka' 'grel dgongs pa rab gsal
Buxa: Nang bstan shes rig 'dzin skyong slob gnyer khang, 1963

Pur-bu-jok (Phur-bu-lcog Byams-pa-rgya-mtsho, 1825–1901)
Explanation of the Presentation of Objects and Object Possessors as well as Awareness and Knowledge in *Magical Key to the Path of Reasoning, Presentation of the Collected Topics Revealing the Meaning of the Treatises on Prime Cognition*
Yul yul can dang blo rig gi rnam par bshad pa *in* Tshad ma'i gzhung don 'byed pa'i bsdus grva'i rnam bzhag rigs lam 'phrul gyi sde mig
Buxa: n.p., 1965

Sa-gya Pandita (Sa-skya Pandi-ta Kun-dga'-rgyal-mtshan, 1182–1251)
Treasury of Reasoning
Tshad ma rigs pa'i gter
The Complete Works of the Great Masters of the Sa-skya Sect of the Tibetan Buddhism, vol. 5, 155.1.1–167.2.1
Tokyo: Toyo Bunko, 1968

Shāntirakṣhita (Zhi-ba-'tsho)
Ornament for the Middle Way
Madhyamakālaṃkāra
dbU ma'i rgyan gyi tshig le'ur byas pa
P5284, vol. 101

Smith, E. Gene
'Introduction' to

Tshad ma rigs pa'i gter gyi rnam par bshad pa rigs pa ma lus pa la 'jug pa'i sgo: A commentary on the Tshad ma rigs gter of Sa-skya paṇḍiṭa, by Glo-bo mkhan-chen Bsod-nams-lhun-grub
Gangtok: S. T. Kazi, n.d.

Sopa, Geshe Lhundup and Hopkins, Jeffrey
Practice and Theory of Tibetan Buddhism
London: Rider, 1976

Stcherbatsky, F. Th.
Buddhist Logic, vol. 2
New York: Dover, 1962

Tsong-ka-pa (Tsong-kha-pa, 1357–1419)
Door of Entry to the Seven Treatises
Sde bdun la 'jug pa'i sgo
The Collected Works of Rje rin po che, vol. 27
New Delhi: Ngawang Gelek Demo, 1977
Golden Rosary of Good Explanation
Legs bshad gser gyi phreng ba
P6150, vol. 154
Ocean of Reasoning, Explanation of (Nāgārjuna's) 'Treatise on the Middle Way'
dbU ma rtsa ba'i tshig le'ur byas pa shes rab ces bya ba'i rnam bshad rigs pa'i rgya mtsho
P6153, vol. 156

Van der Kuijp, L. W. J.
'Phya-Pa Chos-Kyi Seng-Ge's Impact on Tibetan Epistemological Theory'
Journal of Indian Philosophy, vol. 5 (1978), pp. 355–69

Vasubandhu (dbYig-gnyen)
Treasury of Knowledge
Abhidharmakoshakārikā
Chos mngon pa'i mdzod kyi tshig le'ur byas pa
P5590, vol. 115

Wylie, Turrell
'A Standard System of Tibetan Transcription'
HJAS, vol. 22 (1959), pp. 261–7

Notes

1 Ge-shay Jam-bel-sam-pel, *Presentation of Awareness and Knowledge, Composite of all the Important Points, Opener of the Eye of New Intelligence*, modern block-print, n.p., n.d.

2 Pur-bu-jok, *Explanation of the Presentation of Objects and Object-Possessors as well as Awareness and Knowledge* in *Magical Key to the Path of Reasoning, Presentation of the Collected Topics Revealing the Meaning of the Treatises on Prime Cognition* (Buxa: n.p., 1965).

3 Jam-yang-shay-ba, *Presentation of Awareness and Knowledge*, The Collected Works of 'Jam-dbyaṅs-bźad-pa'i-rdo-rje, vol. 15 (New Delhi: Ngawang Gelek Demo, 1973).

4 Turrell Wylie, 'A Standard System of Tibetan Transcriptions', *HJAS*, vol. 22 (1959), pp. 261–7.

5 For example, as explained by Geshe Gedun Lodrö of the University of Hamburg, a Go-mang scholar who was a Visiting Professor at the University of Virginia, Charlottesville from January to August 1979, in the Go-mang College of Dre-bung Monastery beginning students first study 'The Collected Topics of Prime Cognition' for four years; they then study 'Signs and Reasoning' for one year and 'Awareness and Knowledge' for one year. This completes the preliminary phase of their study. Subsequent to this they study the 'Perfections' for five years, 'Madhyamaka' for two years, Vasubandhu's *Treasury of Knowledge* for one year, and 'Discipline' for one year; this completes the second phase of study. The Third phase repeats the topics of the second, but at a more advanced level – another five years of the 'Perfections', two of 'Madhyamaka', and one year of the *Treasury of Knowledge* and 'Discipline' combined. Thus the shortest length of time for completion of the ge-shay studies is twenty-three years, and in fact for the majority of students it takes much longer.

In Dre-bung Monastery's Lo-sel-ling College, the first phase of study was somewhat condensed, with only one year devoted to the study of 'The Collected Topics of Prime Cognition', one year spent on 'Awareness and Knowledge' and one year on 'Signs and Reasoning'. Thus, it was possible to complete the ge-shay studies in a somewhat shorter time, but they nonetheless required eighteen to twenty years.

6 The dates for Dignāga and Dharmakīrti are taken from Masaaki Hattori, *Dignāga, On Perception, being the Pratyakṣapariccheda of Dignāga's 'Pramāṇa-samuccaya' from the Sanskrit Fragments and the Tibetan Versions* (Cambridge, Massachusetts: Harvard University Press, 1968), pp. 4 and 14, who states that he has dated them thus in accordance with E. Frauwallner.

7 Dignāga, *Compendium on Prime Cognition*, P5700, vol. 130.

8 Dharmakīrti, *Commentary on (Dignāga's) 'Compendium on Prime Cognition'*, P5709, vol. 130.

9 Except where noted otherwise, this section on sources and history relies mainly on the oral explanation of Geshe Gedun Lodrö and on his book, *Geschichte der Kloster-Universität Drepung* (Wiesbaden: Franz Steiner, 1974), pp. 232–3.

10 See E. Gene Smith, 'Introduction', to *Tshad ma rigs pa'i gter gyi rnam par bshad pa rigs pa ma lus pa la 'jug pa'i sgo: A Commentary on the Tshad ma rigs gter of Sa-skya paṇḍita*, by Glo-bo mkhan-chen Bsod-nams-lhun-grub (Gangtok: S. T. Kazi, n.d.), pp. 4–5.

11 Sa-gya Paṇḍita, *Treasury of Reasoning*, The Complete Works of the Great Masters of the Sa-skya Sect of the Tibetan Buddhism, vol. 5 (Tokyo: Toyo Bunko, 1968), 155.1.1–167.2.1.

12 Tsong-ka-pa, *Door of Entry to the Seven Treatises*, The Collected Works of Rje rin po che, vol. 27 (New Delhi: Ngawang Gelek Demo, 1977).

13 Kay-drup, *Clearing Away Darkness of Mind with respect to the Seven Treatises (sDe bdun yidkyi mun sel)*. This book has not to the present been reprinted by the Tibetans in India. However Lama Guru Deva is currently engaged in publishing the collected works of Tsong-ka-pa and his spiritual sons, Gyel-tsap and Kay-drup, and thus it should be available within the next year or two.

14 Gen-dun-drup, *Ornament for Valid Reasoning (Tshad ma rigs rgyan)*. This book has also not been reprinted in India and is very difficult to obtain.

15 Pan-chen Sö-nam-drak-ba, *Presentation of Awareness and Knowledge*. I have not been able to locate this book, or even to confirm its existence. Available among the books purchased under PL 480 is his *Illumination of the Thought, Commentary on the Difficult Points of (Dharmakīrti's) 'Commentary on (Dignāga's) "Compendium on Prime Cognition"'* (Buxa: Nang bstan shes rig 'dzin skyong slob gnyer khang, 1963), which served as a major basis for Ge-shay Jam-bel-sam-pel's text.

16 Lo-sang-da-yang, *Investigation of the Limits of Pervasion with Respect to Awareness and Knowledge*, The Collected Works of rJe-btsun bLo-bsaṅ-rta-mgrin, vol. 5 (New Delhi: Lama Guru Deva, 1975).

17 L.W. J. Van de Kuijp, 'Phya-Pa Chos Kyi Seng-Ge's Impact on Tibetan Epistemological Theory', *Journal of Indian Philosophy*, vol. 5 (1978), pp. 358 and 361.

18 The use of the term 'Awareness and Knowledge' (*blo-rig*) to describe the study of consciousness is itself of Tibetan origin. Inasmuch as the three terms, awareness (*blo*), knowledge/knower (*rig pa*), and consciousness (*shes pa*) are synonyms, there seems to be no particular reason for selecting out two of these to describe this area of study. Lati Rinbochay feels that it was probably done primarily for reasons of euphony, with the term for con-

sciousness (*shes pa*) possibly omitted to avoid confusion since there are many Tibetan words with similar pronunciation. Geshe Gedun Lodrö suggested in addition that there might be a loose connection between the usage of 'Awareness and Knowledge' to describe consciousnessess, i.e., 'object-possessors' (*yul can*), and the fact that the definition of 'object' (*yul*) is 'that which an awareness knows'.

19 The source for the Sanskrit of 'subsequent cognizer' and 'awareness to which an object appears but is not ascertained' is F. Th. Stcherbatsky, *Buddhist Logic* (New York: Dover, 1962), vol. 2, pp. 456 and 21; the source for the Sanskrit of 'correctly assuming consciousness' is Sarat Chandra Das, *A Tibetan-English Dictionary* 2nd reprint (Delhi: Motilal Banarsidass, 1970), p. 1135.

20 The Sanskrit for superficial cause of error was constructed in dependence on the Sanskrit supplied for 'superficial error' by Charlene McDermott in 'Direct Sensory Awareness: A Tibetan View and a Medieval Counterpart', *Philosophy East and West*, vol. 23 (1973), p. 347.

21 Tibetan distinguishes between *shes pa* (*jñāna*) and *rnam par shes pa* (*vijñāna*). The first term includes both minds and mental factors whereas the latter refers exclusively to main minds and excludes accompanying mental factors. This difference does not appear to have been made in Sanskrit. For ease of reading, both these terms have been translated as consciousness except in cases where the two are being explicitly contrasted, in which case *shes pa* is translated as consciousness and *rnam par shes pa* as perceiver.

22 Āryadeva is quoted by Jang-gya Rol-bay-dor-jay in 'Prasangika-Madhyamika from *Clear Exposition of the Presentation of Tenets*', translated with commentary by Jeffrey Hopkins, unpublished manuscript, p. 118.

23 There are some scholars who include conceptual meditative consciousnesses within the category of correct assumption and include non-conceptual ones such as those viewing one's surroundings as only water within wrong consciousnesses. See pp. 98–9 and 112–15 above where these two types of consciousness are discussed in more detail along with the reasons why Lati Rinbochay does not feel that it is suitable to call them either correct assumption or wrong consciousnesses.

24 The source for the Sanskrit of 'object of engagement' is Stcherbatsky, p. 361; for 'determined object', Hattori, p. 61; for 'apprehended object', Stcherbatsky, p. 18. The Sanskrit for 'appearing object' was constructed based on Stcherbatsky, p. 456.

25 This term is often translated as valid cognizer. Throughout this text it has been translated as prime cognizer in order to reflect the differing interpretations of it by Sautrāntika and Prāsaṅgika. In Sautrāntika, the first syllable of the Sanskrit word *pramāṇa*, is taken to mean 'new' and thus for them the term means 'to comprehend newly'. In Prāsaṅgika the first syllable is taken to mean 'main' and thus the word means 'that which comprehends its main object'. The translation prime cognizer is used because it is able to encompass both these meanings, whereas valid cognizer gives no suggestion of the meaning 'new'. See pp. 116–19 for a more detailed discussion.

26 This point is not universally accepted. Pur-bu-jok, for example, asserts that only the first moment of inferential cognition is inference; later

moments of that continuum of consciousness are conceptual subsequent cognizers but can no longer be considered inferential ones because they realize their objects not in dependence on a correct sign but merely through the force of the prior moment of consciousness that induced them. Thus, in Pur-bu-jok's system inferential cognizer and inferential prime cognizer are synonymous.

27 It should be noted that with this division of consciousness and with all following ones which are identified as exhaustive, there is the exception of the general category which is neither. For example, although any specific consciousness is either a prime cognizer or a non-prime consciousness, consciousness itself is neither. Although any prime cognizer is necessarily a direct prime cognizer or an inferential prime cognizer, prime cognizer in general is neither a direct nor an inferential prime cognizer. The Tibetans identify this general category as the self-reverse (*rang ldog*) or general reverse (*spyi ldog*).

28 The general sources for this section on eliminative and collective engagers are Den-dar-hla-ram-ba's *Presentation of Specifically and Generally Characterized Phenomena*, the Collected gsung 'bum of Bstan-dar Lha-ram[s] of A-lag-sha, vol. 1 (New Delhi: Lama Guru Deva, 1971) and Na-wang-bel-den's *Explanation of the Meaning of 'Conventional' and 'Ultimate' in the Four Tenet Systems* (New Delhi: Lama Guru Deva, 1972).

29 The term clear can also be taken to refer in this context to the entity of the mind.

30 Another interpretation, in accordance with which this definition has been translated, is that 'clear' refers to the entity of a consciousness and 'knowing' to its function.

31 For those who use this definition, *snang ba* means 'perceive, not 'appear'.

32 This does not mean that the content of non-determinative consciousnesses is non-specific, but that they do not conceptualize, do not engage in the identification, 'This is such and such'.

33 There are four types of relationship that can exist between any two objects:

1 They can be synonymous, as in the case of consciousness and knower, in which case anything that is the one is necessarily the other. This is illustrated by two exactly overlapping circles.

2 They can be contradictory, as in the case of consciousness and matter, in which case there is no one thing which is both. This is illustrated by two circles which do not touch at all.

3 There can be three possibilities between them, as in the case of prime cognizer and consciousness:
(1) anything that is a prime cognizer is necessarily a consciousness, (2) anything that is a consciousness is not necessarily a prime cognizer – for example, a correctly assuming consciousness, and (3) there are things which are neither prime cognizers nor consciousnesses such as a tree. The relationship of three possibilities is illustrated by one circle completely contained within a larger circle.

4 There can be four possibilities between them, as in the case of prime cognizer and self-knower: (1) there is something which is both a prime cognizer and a self-knower such as the first moment of a self-knower

experiencing a sense consciousness apprehending blue, (2) there is something which is neither, such as a subsequent cognizer, (3) there is something which is a prime cognizer but not a self-knower such as the first moment of an eye consciousness apprehending blue, and (4) there is something which is a self-knower but not a prime cognizer such as the second moment of a self-knower experiencing an eye consciousness apprehending blue. This relationship of four possibilities is illustrated by two overlapping circles.

It is an important part of Ge-luk-ba scholastic training to develop the ability to determine which of these relationships exists between objects and is developed by beginning with such relatively easy things as colours, shapes, different types of consciousnesses and then applying this analysis to more and more difficult and abstract topics.

34 For a thorough presentation of the sixteen aspects of the four noble truths, see Jeffrey Hopkins, 'Meditation on Emptiness', unpublished manuscript, Part 3, Chapter 3, pp. 310–34.

35 The reason Ge-shay Jam-bel-sam-pel says, 'It is said . . .', is that this point is not universally accepted among Ge-luk-ba scholars. Jam-yang-shay-ba, for example, holds that the only type of mental direct perceiver is that produced at the end of a continuum of sense perception – i.e., that explicitly indicated by Dignāga and Dharmakīrti. Other types of consciousnesses such as clairvoyances, self-knowers, and yogic direct perceivers are, for him, mental consciousnesses and are directly perceiving ones, but are not mental direct perceivers.

36 Saying 'stable predispositions' distinguishes between consciousnesses which are polluted by a superficial cause of error and those which are not. The predispositions which give rise to direct perceivers are stable in the sense that their continuum will continue as long as does cyclic existence; those that give rise to wrong consciousnesses such as a sense consciousness seeing blue snow mountains or a thought apprehending sound as permanent are unstable in that their continuum can be adventitiously cut off.

37 For a discussion of true and false aspectarian Chittamātrins. see Geshe Lhundup Sopa and Jeffrey Hopkins, *Practice and Theory of Tibetan Buddhism*, (London: Rider, 1976), pp. 107–8.

38 This argument hinges on the difference between a syllogism and a consequence, which can be illustrated by an example. A correct syllogism proving sound to be impermanent is, 'The subject, sound, is impermanent because of being a product'. In this case the sign in dependence on which sound is being realized to be impermanent is that it is a product; in dependence on it one could generate an inferential cognizer realizing sound to be impermanent. However, someone who strongly holds an opposite view, i.e., that sound is permanent, will not at once accept this, and thus it is necessary to first break down the force of that wrong view by stating to the opponent a consequence which demonstrates a contradiction in that opponent's position. Thus, to a Sāṃkhya who holds that sound is permanent, sound is a product, and that whatever is a product is impermanent, one would state the consequence, 'It follows that the subject, sound, is not a product because of being permanent'. This is not a correct statement, but

is stated thus to cause the opponent to see the contradiction in his position. This contradictory consequence implies the syllogism, 'The subject, sound, is impermanent because of being a product'. The controversy is over whether it is necessary actually to state that syllogism or whether someone could generate an inferential cognizer merely in dependence on the consequence. For a more extensive discussion of the steps involved in causing someone to generate an inferring consciousness see Jeffrey Hopkins. 'Meditation on Emptiness', Appendix 3, Proof Statements, pp. 775–81.

39 The text was corrected from *mi rtogs* to *mi rtag rtogs*, p. 5b.1.

40 This has been identified by Geshe Gedun Lodrö as Dharmottara's *Commentary on (Dharmakīrti's) 'Ascertainment of Prime Cognition'*, P5727, vol. 136.

41 However, this objection is primarily a play on words as it is very difficult actually to posit any correctly assuming consciousness which is, in fact, the effect of experience.

42 The Tibetan of this is *sha pa,* which is an abbreviation for *shim-sha-pa,* a transliteration of the Sanskrit *shiṃshapā,* which Monier-Williams identifies as the Dalbergia Sissoo or Ashoka tree in his *Sanskrit-English Dictionary,* fifth reprint (Delhi: Motilal Banarsidass, 1976), p. 1069.

43 The text was corrected from *lta bu* to *lta ba,* p. 12a.2.

Index

A-gya-yong-dzin (A-kya-yongs-'dzin), 145
alternating production, 56-7
appearing object, 25, 28-9, 33, 47, 51, 102-5, 134
apprehended (*grāhya, bzung ba*), 60
apprehended object, 28-9, 102-4, 111-12
apprehender (*grāhaka, 'dzin pa*), 60
Āryadeva, 24
Asaṅga, 12
ascertaining consciousness, 106
ascertainment, 23, 34-5
awareness to which the object appears but is not ascertained, 14, 23, 31, 34, 61, 69, 83, 85, 102-9, 127

basis, 21, 23, 33-4, 35, 51, 63, 64, 75, 93
bliss, 107
Bodhisattva, 44, 108, 114-15
Buddha, 44, 46, 65-6, 108, 113-14, 117, 118, 134, 142

calm abiding, 20, 62, 88-9
cause and effect of actions, 78, 100
Cha-ba-chö-gi-seng-gay (Cha-pa-chos-kyi-seng-ge), 12, 14
Chandrakīrti, 113
Chittamātra, 15, 19, 45, 64, 65, 66, 70-1, 75, 117, 134, 138, 139, 165
clairvoyance, 19, 54-5, 57, 59, 72, 165
clear appearance, 27, 31, 64, 89, 112-13
clear light, 11, 46, 64
Clearing Away Darkness of Mind with Respect to the Seven Treatises, 13, 58, 87
Collected Topics of Prime Cognition (bsDus sgrva), 13
collective engager, 34, 132, 141-2
Commentary on (Dignāga's) 'Compendium on Prime Cognition' (Pramānavarttika), 12, 45, 73, 108, 112, 118, 119
compassion, 28, 99
Compendium of Knowledge (Abhidharmasamuchchaya), 12

Compendium on Prime Cognition (Pramāṇasamuchchaya), 12, 72
conceptual consciousnesses, 16, 21, 24, 27, 29, 33, 34, 50-1, 66-7, 68, 85-6, 102-3, 109, 111, 130-2, 136, 141
consciousness arisen from hearing, 92-3, 130-1
consequence, 75, 83-4, 165-6
contextual prime cognizer, 120
conventional prime cognizer, 123
The Correct, 86, 166
correct sign, 21, 75-6, 78, 94, 99, 136, 165-6
correctly assuming consciousness, 14, 22-3, 26, 92-9, 120, 135
counter pervasion, 73, 83, 97-8

denying consciousness, 132
determinative knower, 50, 76, 164
determined object, 28-9, 102-4, 109
Dharmakīrti, 12, 13, 14, 45, 73, 108, 112-14, 118, 119, 162
Dharmottara, 57, 86, 117, 166
Dignāga, 12, 14, 72, 74, 162
direct perceiver, 14, 16-20, 27-8, 29-30, 31, 34, 47, 50-74, 85, 94, 103-4, 111-12, 120, 134, 135
direct prime cognizer, 121, 135 (*see also* prime cognizer; direct perceiver)
directly realize, 124, 137
Door of Entry to the Seven Treatises, 13
doubting consciousness, 14, 24, 26, 93, 99-102, 132
dream consciousness, 110, 112
Dza-ri-ga-ba (Tsa-ri-ka-pa), 119, 120-1

earth-totality meditation, 28, 112-15, 163
eliminative engager, 34-5, 132, 141-2
empowering condition, 68
emptiness, 45-6, 100 (*see also* selflessness)
enlightment, 11, 25-6, 35
enumeration of prime cognizers, 32, 118-21
exalted knower of all aspects (*see* omniscience)
experience, 22, 94-6, 98-9

facsimiles of direct perception, 72-4
factually concordant thought consciousness, 102, 111, 131
factually discordant thought consciousness, 102, 111, 131
Four Hundred (Chatuhshataka), 24
free from conceptuality, 16, 23, 49-50, 65

Ga-dam-ba (bKa'-gdams-pa), 12
Ge-luk-ba (dGe-lugs-pa), 11, 13, 18, 26, 161, 165
ge-shay training, 11-12, 161
Gen-dun-drup (dGe-'dun-grub), 13
generally characterized phenomenon, 119
Go-mang College, 13, 161
Golden Rosary of Good Explanation, 114

Gön-chok-jik-may-wang-bo (dKon-mchog-'jigs-med-dbang-po), 65
great compassion, 28, 44, 99
Gyel-tsap (rGyal-tshab), 56, 59, 87

hidden phenomenon, 59, 69, 120

immediately preceding condition, 17, 51, 67-71
impermanence, 20, 34, 67, 78, 82-4, 88-90, 93, 96-8, 108, 135-6, 165-6
impermanent phenomenon, 11, 30-1, 47, 104
implicit realization, 47, 124
inattentive mind, 128
incontrovertible, 21, 22, 23, 27, 31, 51, 52, 76, 78, 91, 117
indicated on this occasion, 54-7
inference by the power of the fact, 77, 81-2, 121
inference for another, 83
inference for oneself, 83
inference through belief, 69, 77-80, 121
inference through example, 120, 121
inference through renown, 77, 80-81, 121
inferential cognizer, 14, 20-2, 26-7, 51, 73, 75-84, 94, 106-7, 163-4
inferential prime cognizer, 76, 106-7, 119, 136, 164
initial direct perceiver, 128
intermediate state, 55
introspection, 19

Jainas, 120
Jam-yang-shay-ba ('Jam-dbyangs-bzhad-pa), 7, 13, 14, 59, 62, 64, 67, 88, 96, 108, 125-6, 130, 141-2, 165
Jay-dzun-ba (rJe-rtsun-pa), 76, 79, 125-6, 141-2

Kay-drup (mKhas-grub), 13, 58, 79, 87, 113, 114

locus of mind, 139-40
Lo-sang-da-yang (bLo-bzang-rta-dbyangs), 14
Lo-sang-drak-ba (bLo-bzang-grags-pa), 44 (*see also* Tsong-ka-pa)
Lo-sel-ling College, 13, 14, 161

Mādhyamika, 15, 19, 45, 75, 113, 123
Mahāyāna mind-generation, 114-15
manifest phenomenon, 78-80
Mañjughoṣha, 44
Mañjushrī, 44
meaning generality, 21, 29-30, 35, 50-51, 67, 98, 103, 111, 130, 135, 141
meditative stabilization on ugliness, 99, 112-15
mental consciousness, 33, 134 (*see also* mental direct perceivers)
mental direct perceivers, 18-19, 54-9, 61, 65, 66, 68, 69, 71, 85, 106
mental factors, 35-9, 99-101
mental perceiver, 36, 134-5, 139
mind apprehending a sign, 72-3

minds and mental factors, 12, 15, 35-6, 99-101, 134-5, 138, 142-5
mistaken consciousness, 21, 25, 33, 111-15, 133-4
monastic education, 11-12, 161, 165

Naiyāyikas, 120
naming, 80-1, 131
nature of mind, 11, 15, 46, 140
negative phenomenon, 29, 35, 45, 67, 84-5
new realization, 32, 87-8, 117-18
Nihilist, 106-7, 109, 110, 119-20
non-affirming negative, 67
non-conceptual consciousness, 16, 28, 30-1, 33, 34, 49-50, 110, 111-112, 132-3
non-mistaken, 16, 23, 33, 51, 134
non-prime consciousness, 32, 84, 128-9
non-realizing awareness, 132

object of comprehension, 51, 119, 121, 122, 126
object of engagement, 25, 28-9, 33, 51, 93, 102-5
object of the mode of apprehension, 103
observed object condition, 17, 53, 66-71, 138
obstructions, 44, 90
Ocean of Reasoning, Explanation of (Nāgārjuna's) 'Treatise on the Middle Way', 110
omniscience, 64-6, 78, 87-8, 90, 108, 118, 142
one casual collection, 62
Ornament for the Middle Way (Madhyamakālamkāra), 45
Ornament for Valid Reasoning, 13
other-knower, 55-6, 59, 62-3

Pan-chen Sö-nam-drak-ba (Pan-chen bSod-nams-grags-pa), 13, 46, 56, 59, 73, 77, 79, 108, 125-6, 137, 141-2, 145
permanent phenomenon, 29-31, 47, 67, 103-4, 105
pervasion, 21, 73, 83, 97-8
pliancy, 107
positive phenomenon, 45, 84-5
Prajñākaragupta, 57
pramāṇa, 31-2, 116-18, 163 (*see also* prime cognizer)
Prāsaṅgika-Mādhyamika, 19, 64, 71, 75, 117-18, 121, 138, 139
predispositions, 34, 65, 70, 81, 138, 165
presence of the reason in the subject, 73, 83, 97-8
prime cognizer, 31-2, 61, 76, 78, 84, 86-90, 117-29, 135, 163, 164
prime cognizers that induce ascertainment by themselves, 121-5
prime cognizers when ascertainment is induced by another, 121-2, 123, 125-8
production of three types, 56-8
production only at the end of the continuum, 18, 56-8
proof for omniscience, 64
proof for yogic direct perceiver, 63-4
proof statement, 83-4
Pur-bu-jok (Phur-bu-lcog), 7, 14, 62, 66, 76, 130, 141-2, 145, 163

Ra-dö (Rva-stod), 73, 93, 100, 141, 145
reasoning, 21, 22, 26-8, 35, 64, 69
root afflictions, 37-8, 100-1, 144

Sa-gya Pandita (Sa-skya Paṇḍita), 13, 14, 57, 98, 125, 127
sameness in establishment and abiding, 86
Sāṃkhya, 83-4, 107, 120, 165
Sautrāntika, 12, 15, 19, 30-1, 37, 45, 47, 64, 65, 66, 75, 104, 113, 117, 122, 124, 134, 138, 139, 144
Sautrāntika-Svātantrika-Mādhyamika, 19, 64, 138, 139
scriptural inference, 69, 121
self-knower (*see* self-knowing direct perceiver)
self-knowing direct perceiver, 19, 49, 59-61, 62-3, 64, 65, 67, 68, 71-2, 94, 106-7, 125, 165
self-reverse, 50, 105, 164
selflessness, 20, 25, 26-8, 47, 66-7, 78, 90, 124, 135
sense consciousness, 33-4, 65, 137 (*see also* sense direct perceivers)
sense direct perceivers, 17-18, 52-54, 65, 67, 68, 70, 71, 106, 123-4, 125-6
sense direct prime cognizer having a familiar object, 18, 122-4
sense direct prime cognizer to which the ability to perform a function appears, 18, 82, 124
sense perceivers, 36, 138, 139, 143, 163 (*see also* sense consciousness; sense direct perceivers)
sense power, 33-4, 47, 53-4, 63, 68, 137
Shaṅkarānanda, 57
Shāntirakṣhita, 45
sign, 21, 22 (*see also* correct sign)
sign by the power of the fact, 78
sign of belief, 78
sign of renown, 80
similarity of reverse type, 58-9
similarity of substantial type, 58-9
slightly hidden phenomenon, 78-80
sound generality, 50-51, 92, 130
special insight, 20, 62, 90
specifically characterized phenomenon, 30-1, 102, 105, 111, 119
states arisen from hearing, 92-3, 130-1
states arisen from meditation, 54-5, 89, 94, 98-9, 130-1
states arisen from thinking/thought, 90, 130-1
subsequent cognizer, 14, 22, 27, 32, 61, 76, 84-91
superficial cause of error, 16, 51-2, 112, 114, 165
superimposing consciousness, 113-15, 128, 132
superimpositions, 22, 52, 90-1, 93
Superior (Ārya), 18, 20, 62, 104, 134
Supplement to the Middle Way (Madhyamakāvatāra), 113
sūtra, 54, 57, 113-14
Svātantrika-Mādhyamika, 19, 64, 65, 75, 117, 138, 139
syllogism, 78, 84, 165-6

terminological suitability, 81
that which has the aspect of the apprehended (*grāhya-ākāra, bzung rnam*), 60
that which has the aspect of the apprehender (*grāhaka-ākāra, 'dzin rnam*), 60
thought, 30, 34, 35, 50, 109 (*see also* conceptual consciousnesses)
thought consciousness affixing names, 131
thought consciousness affixing the meaning, 131
three modes, 73, 83, 97-8
transformation of consciousness, 26-8
Treasury of Knowledge (Abhidharmakosha), 37, 64
Treasury of Reasoning, 13, 57, 98, 125, 127-8
Tsong-ka-pa (Tsong-kha-pa), 13, 44, 56, 59, 110, 114

uncommon empowering condition, 17, 20, 33-4, 53, 54, 62-3, 68-71, 134, 137, 139, 143
unreal mental application, 113-14

Vaibhāṣhika, 15, 17, 19, 37, 45, 47, 64, 68, 117, 138, 139, 144
Vaisheṣhika, 16, 49, 107, 110, 120
valid persons and scriptures, 117
Vasubandhu, 37, 64
very hidden phenomenon, 59, 69, 77-80

water-totality meditation, 28, 112-15, 163
wrong consciousness, 14, 21, 24-5, 26, 33, 60, 95, 104-5, 109-10, 111-15, 165
wrong ideas, 132

Yogāchāra-Svātantrika-Mādhyamika, 19, 64, 65, 138, 139
yogic direct perceivers, 19-20, 31, 56, 61-5, 66-7, 68, 71, 89-90, 107-8, 113, 124, 125, 137, 165

Tibetan Text

༄༅། །བློ་རིག་གི་རྣམ་བཞག་ཉེར་མཁོ་ཀུན་འདུས་བློ་གསར་མིག་འབྱེད་ཅེས་བྱ་བ་བཞུགས་སོ། །

༄༅། །བློ་གཏེར་འཇམ་དཔལ་དབྱངས་ཉིད་སྨྲ་བའི
བཞག་ཉེར་མཁོ་ཀུན་འདུས་པས། །བློ་དམན་རིག་པའི་སྣང་བ་རྒྱས་ཕྱིར་
ཉིད། དབྱེ་བ། དབྱེ་བ་སོ་སོའི་དོན་བཤད་པའོ། །༈ དང་པོ་ནི། རིག་པ

གས། །ཕྱོགས་བཅད་གྲགས་པའི་དཔལ་ལ་ཕྱག་འཚལ་ནས། །བློ་རིག་རྣམ་
ཕྱེལ། །དེ་ལ་འདིར་བློ་རིག་གི་རྣམ་བཞག་བཤད་པ་ལ་གསུམ། །མཚན
བློའི་མཚན་ཉིད། གསལ་ཞིང་རིག་པ་ཤེས་པའི་མཚན་ཉིད། །བློ་དང་

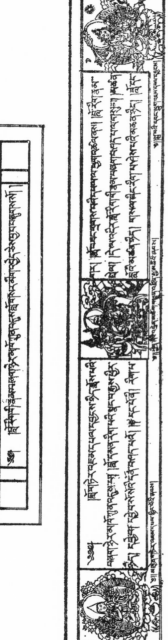

༄༅། །རིག་པ་ཤེས་པ་གསུམ་དོན་གཅིག །༈ གཉིས་པ་དབྱེ་བ་ལ་གསུམ། བློ་རིག་བདུན་དུ་དབྱེ་བ། བློ་རིག་གསུམ་དུ་དབྱེ་བ། བློ་རིག་གཉིས་སུ་
དབྱེ་བའོ། །༈ དང་པོ་ཡོད་དེ། མངོན་སུམ། རྗེས་དཔག །བཅད་ཤེས། ཡིད་དཔྱོད། སྣང་ལ་མ་ངེས། ཐེ་ཚོམ། ལོག་ཤེས་དང་བདུན་ཡོད་པའི་ཕྱིར། །༈ གསུམ་པ་…
དབྱེ་བ་སོ་སོའི་དོན་ལ་བདུན། །དང་པོ་མངོན་སུམ་བཤད་པ་ལ་མཚན་ཉིད་དང་། །དབྱེ་བ་གཉིས། རྟོག་པ་དང་བྲལ་ཞིང་མ་འཁྲུལ་བའི་རིག་པ་མངོན་སུམ་གྱི་མཚན་ཉིད། རྟོག་པ་དང་

བྲལ་ཞིང་མ་འཁྲུལ་བའི་གསར་དུ་མི་བསླུ་བའི་རིག་པ་མངོན་སུམ་གྱི་ཚད་མའི་མཚན་ཉིད། དེ་ལ་དབྱེ་ན། དབང་མངོན། ཡིད་མངོན། རང་རིག་མངོན་སུམ། རྣལ་འབྱོར་མངོན་སུམ་དང་བཞི། རང་གི་ཐུན་མོང་
མ་ཡིན་པའི་བདག་རྐྱེན་དབང་པོ་གཟུགས་ཅན་པ་ལས་སྐྱེས་པའི་རྟོག་པ་དང་བྲལ་ཞིང་མ་འཁྲུལ་བའི་རིག་པ་དབང་མངོན་གྱི་མཚན་ཉིད། དབྱེ་ན། གཟུགས་འཛིན་དབང་མངོན། སྒྲ་འཛིན་དབང་མངོན། དྲི་འཛིན་…
དབང་མངོན། རོ་འཛིན་དབང་མངོན། རེག་བྱ་འཛིན་པའི་དབང་མངོན་དང་ལྔ། །༈ [illegible] མ་ཡིན་པའི་བདག་རྐྱེན་མིག་དབང་དང་། དམིགས་རྐྱེན་གཟུགས་ལ་བརྟེན་ནས་སྐྱེས་པའི་རྟོག་པ་དང་བྲལ་…
ཞིང་མ་འཁྲུལ་བའི་རིག་པ། གཟུགས་འཛིན་དབང་མངོན་གྱི་མཚན་ཉིད། དེས་[illegible]་རིགས་འགྲེ། །༈ རང་གི་ཐུན་མོང་མ་ཡིན་པའི་བདག་རྐྱེན་ཡིད་དབང་ལས་སྐྱེས་པའི་རྟོག་པ་དང་བྲལ་ཞིང་མ་…

Tibetan Texts 1–4

ཀ། གསུམ [illegible]

༄། །འཁྲུལ་བའི་རིགས་པ། ཡིད་མངོན་གྱི་མཚན་ཉིད། དེ་ལ་དབྱེ་ན། སྐབས་འདིར་བསྟན་གྱི་ཡིད་མངོན་དང་། དེ་མ་ཡིན་པའི་ཡིད་མངོན་གཉིས། རང་གི་ཐུན་མོང་མ་ཡིན་པའི་བདག་རྐྱེན་
ཡིད་དབང་ལས་བྱུང་བའི་སྐབས་འདིར་བསྟན་གྱི་རྟོག་བྲལ་མ་འཁྲུལ་བའི་གཞན་རིག་དང་པོའི་མཚན་ཉིད། དབྱེ་ན། གཟུགས་འཛིན་ཡིད་མངོན་ནས་རེག་བྱ་འཛིན་པའི་ཡིད་མངོན་གྱི་བར་ལྔ། སྐབས་འདིར་བསྟན་
གྱི་ཡིད་མངོན་སྐྱེ་ཚུལ་ལ། སྤེལ་མར་སྐྱེ་བ། འགྲོས་གསུམ་པར་སྐྱེ་བ། རྒྱུན་མཐའ་མ་ཁོ་ནར་སྐྱེ་བ་དང་འདོད་ཚུལ་གསུམ་ལས། དང་པོའི་ཚུལ་ནི། གཟུགས་འཛིན་དབང་མངོན་སྐད་ཅིག་དང་པོ་སྐྱེ། དེའི་རྗེས་སུ་གཟུགས་
འཛིན་ཡིད་མངོན་སྐད་ཅིག་དང་པོ་སྐྱེས། དེའི་རྗེས་སུ་གཟུགས་འཛིན་དབང་མངོན་སྐད་ཅིག་གཉིས་པ་སྐྱེ་བ་སོགས་དབང་མངོན་སྐད་ཅིག་རེ་རེའི་བར་ཡིད་མངོན་སྐད་ཅིག་རེ་སྐྱེ་བར་འདོད། གཉིས་པའི་ཚུལ་

ནི་གཟུགས་འཛིན་དབང་མངོན་སྐད་ཅིག་གཉིས་པ་དང་། གཟུགས་འཛིན་ཡིད་མངོན་སྐད་ཅིག་དང་པོ། དེ་གཉིས་ཉམས་སུ་མྱོང་བའི་རང་རིག་མངོན་སུམ་དང་གསུམ་དུས་མཉམ་དུ་སྐྱེ་བར་འདོད་པ་སྟེ། མདོར་ན་ཁ་ཕྱིར་ལྟས་ཀྱི་འགྲོས་
གཉིས་དང་ཁ་ནང་ལྟས་ཀྱི་འགྲོས་གཅིག་ཅིག་ཆར་དུ་སྐྱེ་བར་འདོད། གསུམ་པའི་ཚུལ་ནི། རྗེ་ཡབ་སྲས་ཀྱི་དགོངས་པ། གཟུགས་འཛིན་དབང་མངོན་སྐད་ཅིག་ཐ་མའི་མཇུག་ཐོགས་ཁོ་ནར་གཟུགས་འཛིན་ཡིད་མངོན་སྐྱེ་བར་བཞེད།
དེ་ཡང་ཚུར་མཐོང་གི་རྒྱུད་ལ་ནི་གཟུགས་འཛིན་ཡིད་མངོན་དུས་མཐའི་སྐད་ཅིག་མ་རེ་རེ་ལས་མི་སྐྱེ་བར་འདོད་དགོས་པར་ཡིག་ཆར་གསལ་ལོ། །སྐབས་འདིར་བསྟན་ཞེས་པ། གཞུང་ཤེས་པ་ནི་རྣམ་གཉིས་ཏེ། མིག་དང་ཡིད་ལ་
བརྟེན་པའོ། །ཞེས་པའི་སྐབས་ལ་བཀོད་དགོས་སོ། །གཉིས་པ་ནི་གཞན་སེམས་ཤེས་པའི་མངོན་ཤེས་ལྟ་བུའོ། །༈ འཛིན་རྣམ་རང་རིག་གི་མཚན་ཉིད། རྟོག་པ་དང་བྲལ་ཞིང་མ་འཁྲུལ་བའི་འཛིན་རྣམ་རང་རིག་མངོན་སུམ་གྱི་མཚན་

ཀ། བཞི [illegible]

༄། །ཉིད། དབྱེ་ན། དེར་གྱུར་པའི་ཚད་མ། བཅད་ཤེས། སྣང་ལ་མ་ངེས་དང་གསུམ། །༈ རང་གི་ཐུན་མོང་མ་ཡིན་པའི་བདག་རྐྱེན་དུ་གྱུར་པའི་ཞི་ལྷག་ཟུང་འབྲེལ་གྱི་ཏིང་ངེ་འཛིན་ལས་སྐྱེས་པའི་རྟོག་བྲལ་མ་
འཁྲུལ་བའི་འཕགས་རྒྱུད་ཀྱི་མཁྱེན་པ་རྣལ་འབྱོར་མངོན་སུམ་གྱི་མཚན་ཉིད། དབྱེ་ན། ཉན་ཐོས། རང་རྒྱལ། ཐེག་ཆེན་གྱི་དེ་གསུམ་ཡོད། རང་རིག་མངོན་སུམ་དང་། རྣལ་འབྱོར་མངོན་སུམ་ལ་ཡིད་མངོན་ཡིན་དགོས་པར་
གསུངས། མཚན་ཉིད་དེ་རྣམས་མདོ་སྡེ་པའི་དབང་དུ་བྱས་ཀྱི་སེམས་ཙམ་པ་དང་། རྣལ་འབྱོར་སྤྱོད་པའི་དབུ་མ་པ་རྣམས་ཀྱིས། རྟོག་པ་དང་བྲལ་ཞིང་བག་ཆགས་བརྟན་བྱུང་གི་རིག་པ་ཞེས་སྦྱར་རོ། །ཞར་བྱུང་མངོན་སུམ་ལྟར་སྣང་གི་རྣམ་
བཞག་ཅུང་ཟད་བཤད་པ་ལ། འཁྲུལ་དང་ཀུན་རྫོབ་ཤེས་པ་དང་། །རྗེས་དཔག་རྗེས་སུ་དཔག་ལས་བྱུང་། དྲན་དང་མངོན་འདོད་ཅེས་བྱ་བ། མངོན་སུམ་ལྟར་སྣང་རབ་རིབ་བཅས། ཅེས་གསུངས་པ་ལྟར། རྟོག་པ་མངོན་སུམ་ལྟར་སྣང་

དྲུག་རྟོག་མེད་མངོན་སུམ་ལྟར་སྣང་གཅིག་དང་བདུན་དུ་འདོད། རྣམ་འགྲེལ་རྩ་བས་དེ་དག་བཞིར་བསྡུས་ནས་བཤད་དོ། །འདི་དག་ཞིབ་ཏུ་ཤེས་པར་འདོད་ན་[illegible]་རིག་དང་ལེའུ་གསུམ་པའི་དགོངས་པ་རབ་གསལ་ལ་སོགས་ལ་ལྟ་བར་བྱའོ། །
༈ རང་གི་རྟེན་རྟགས་ཡང་དག་ལ་བརྟེན་ནས་རང་གི་གཞལ་བྱ་ལྐོག་གྱུར་ལ་མི་བསླུ་བའི་ཞེན་རིག་རྗེས་དཔག་གི་མཚན་ཉིད། རང་གི་རྟེན་རྟགས་ཡང་དག་ལ་བརྟེན་ནས་རང་གི་གཞལ་བྱ་ལྐོག་གྱུར་ལ་གསར་དུ་མི་བསླུ་བའི་རིག་པ། རྗེས་
དཔག་ཚད་མའི་མཚན་ཉིད། རྗེས་དཔག་ལ་ཚད་མས་མ་ཁྱབ་པར་གསུངས། དེ་ལ་དབྱེ་ན། ཡིད་ཆེས་རྗེས་དཔག །གྲགས་པའི་རྗེས་དཔག །དངོས་སྟོབས་རྗེས་དཔག་དང་གསུམ། རང་གི་རྟེན་ཡིད་ཆེས་ཀྱི་རྟགས་ཡང་དག་ལ་བརྟེན་
ནས་རང་གི་གཞལ་བྱ་ཤིན་ཏུ་ལྐོག་གྱུར་ལ་མི་བསླུ་བའི་ཞེན་རིག་དང་པོའི་མཚན་ཉིད། མཚན་གཞི་ནི། སྦྱིན་པས་ལོངས་སྤྱོད་ཁྲིམས་ཀྱིས་བདེ། ཞེས་པའི་ལུང་རང་གི་བསྟན་བྱའི་དོན་ལ་མི་བསླུ་བར་རྟོགས་པའི་རྗེས་དཔག་ལྟ་བུ། རང་གི་རྟེན་གྲགས་

༄༅། ། རྟགས་ཡང་དག་ལ་བརྟེན་ནས་རང་གི་གཞལ་བྱ་ལྐོག་གྱུར་ལ་མི་བསླུ་བའི་ཞེན་རིག་གསར་པའི་མཚན་ཉིད། མཚན་གཞི། རི་བོང་ཅན་ལ་ཟླ་བ་ཞེས་པའི་སྒྲས་བརྗོད་རུང་དུ་རྟོགས་པའི་རྗེས་དཔག་ལྟ་བུ། རང་གི
རྟེན་དངོས་སྟོབས་ཀྱི་རྟགས་ཡང་དག་ལ་བརྟེན་ནས་རང་གི་གཞལ་བྱ་ལྐོག་གྱུར་ལ་མི་བསླུ་བའི་ཞེན་རིག་གསུམ་པའི་མཚན་ཉིད། མཚན་གཞི། སྒྲ་མི་རྟག་རྟོགས་ཀྱི་རྗེས་དཔག་ལྟ་བུའོ། །རང་འགྲེན་བྱེད་ཀྱི་ཚད་མ་སྔ་མས
རྟོགས་ཟིན་རྟོགས་པའི་ཚད་མིན་གྱི་རིག་པ་བཅད་ཤེས་ཀྱི་མཚན་ཉིད། དེ་ལ་དབྱེ་ན། མངོན་སུམ་བཅད་ཤེས་དང་རྟོག་པ་བཅད་ཤེས་གཉིས། དང་པོ་ལ་དབང་མངོན་བཅད་ཤེས། ཡིད་མངོན་བཅད་ཤེས། རང་རིག་བཅད་ཤེས། རྣལ་
འབྱོར་མངོན་སུམ་བཅད་ཤེས་དང་བཞི། གཉིས་པ་ལ་མངོན་སུམ་གྱིས་དྲངས་པའི་རྟོག་པ་བཅད་ཤེས་དང་། རྗེས་དཔག་གིས་དྲངས་པའི་རྟོག་པ་བཅད་ཤེས་གཉིས། མཚན་གཞི། སྔོ་འཛིན་མངོན་སུམ་གྱི་རྗེས་སུ་སྐྱེས་པའི་སྔོན་པོ

ངེས་པའི་ངེས་ཤེས་ལྟ་བུ་དང་པོ་དང་། སྒྲ་མི་རྟག་རྟོགས་ཀྱི་རྗེས་དཔག་སྐད་ཅིག་གཉིས་པ་ལྟ་བུ་གཉིས་པ་ཡིན་པའི་ཕྱིར་ཏེ། འཐད་ལྡན་ལས། མངོན་སུམ་དང་རྗེས་སུ་དཔག་པའི་དང་པོ་སྐད་ཅིག་མ་གཉིས་ནི་ཚད་མ་ཡིན་ལ་དེ
དག་གི་རྒྱུན་དུ་གྱུར་པའི་ཤུགས་པ་དང་བཅད་པ་ཐ་མི་དད་པ་ཕྱི་མ་རྣམས་ནི་ཚད་མ་མ་ཡིན་པར་བཞེད་པའོ། །ཞེས་གསུངས་པའི་ཕྱིར། མཁས་པ་འདིའི་ལུགས་བདེ་བ་གཅིག་པ་འབྲས་བུ་གཅིག་པ་ལ་བྱེད་པ་གསུངས། །རང་གི་འཇུག་ཡུལ
གྱི་ཆོས་ལ་ཞུགས་པའི་ཆོས་ལ་མཐར་གཅིག་ཏུ་ཞེན་ཀྱང་བཅད་དོན་མ་ཐོབ་པའི་རིག་པ་ཡིད་དཔྱོད་ཀྱི་མཚན་ཉིད། དེ་ལ་དབྱེ་ན། རྒྱུ་མཚན་མེད་པའི་ཡིད་དཔྱོད། རྒྱུ་མཚན་མ་ངེས་པའི་ཡིད་དཔྱོད། རྒྱུ་མཚན་ལྟར་སྣང་ལ་བརྟེན
པའི་ཡིད་དཔྱོད་དང་གསུམ། མཚན་གཞི་ནི། རྒྱུ་མཚན་གང་ཡང་མེད་པར་སྒྲ་མི་རྟག་རྟོགས་པའི་བློ་ལྟ་བུ་དང་པོ་དང་། སྒྲ་བྱས་པ་དང་། བྱས་ན་མི་རྟག་པས་ཁྱབ་པ་མ་ངེས་པར་བྱས་པའི་རྟགས་ལས་སྒྲ་མི་རྟག་རྟོགས་པའི་བློ་ལྟ་བུ་གཉིས་པ

༄༅། །དང་། གཞལ་བྱའི་རྟགས་ལས་སྒྲ་མི་རྟག་རྟོགས་པའི་བློ་ལྟ་བུ་གསུམ་པ་ཡིན་པའི་ཕྱིར། དེ་ཕྱིར་ཡང་། རིགས་གཏེར་ལས། ཡིད་དཔྱོད་རྒྱུ་ལ་བརྟེན་མི་རྟོགས། དམ་བཅའ་ཙམ་ཡིན་ཟེ་ཚོམ་འགྱུར། རྟགས་ལ་བརྟེན་ན་ཡང
དག་གམ། ལྟར་སྣང་གསུམ་ལས་འདའ་བ་མེད། ཅེས་གསུངས། ཡང་ན། སྒྲོ་བ་དང་རྟེན་ཏེ་ཡང་དག་གང་རུང་ལ་མ་བརྟེན་པར་རང་གི་འཇུག་ཡུལ་ལ་མ་འཁྲུལ་བའི་མཐར་གཅིག་འཛིན་གྱི་བཅད་དོན་མ་ཐོབ་པའི་ཞེན་རིག །དེའི
མཚན་ཉིད་དུ་འཇོག །དེ་ནི་སྐྱོང་བ་ལ་སྐོམ་ཕྱུང་གི་སྐྱོང་བ་དང་། རང་རིག་གི་སྐྱོང་བ་དང་། དོན་ཕྱི་དང་མཐུན་པའི་གསལ་བ་སྐྱོང་གསུམ་དུ་ཡོད་པའི། ཀུན་ལ་ཡང་མ་བརྟེན་པར་བྱ་དགོས་པས། དེ་ལྟར་ན་བློ་ཡིན་ན་བློ་རིག་བདུན་པོ་གང་
རུང་ཡིན་པས་མ་ཁྱབ་པར་སེམས་ཏེ། མི་རྟག་པའི་རྟེན་དེ་འཛིན་དང་། སྟོབས་པའི་རྒྱུད་ཀྱི་སྙིང་རྗེ་ཆེན་པོ་སོགས་ཐབས་ཀྱི་རྟོགས་རིགས་སུ་གནས་པ་རྣམས། གཞན་རྣམས་མིན་པར་གོ་སླ་ལ། སེམས་བྱུང་གི་སྐྱོང་བ་ལ་རྩོས་པས་ཡོད

དཔྱོད་དུ་མི་རིགས། འགྲུབ་ལ་རྒྱུས་མ་ཤད་པས་ལོག་ཤེས་སུ་མི་རིགས་པའི་ཕྱིར་རྣམ་རྟེ་དཔྱད་པར་བྱའོ། །རང་སྟོབས་ཀྱིས་མཐའ་གཉིས་སུ་དོགས་པའི་རིག་པ་ཐེ་ཚོམ་གྱི་མཚན་ཉིད། དེ་ལ་དབྱེ་ན། དོན་འགྱུར་གྱི་ཐེ་ཚོམ། དོན་མི
འགྱུར་གྱི་ཐེ་ཚོམ། ཆ་མཉམ་པའི་ཐེ་ཚོམ་དང་གསུམ། མཚན་གཞི་ནི། སྒྲ་ཕལ་ཆེར་མི་རྟག་གམ་སྙམ་པའི་ཡིད་གཉིས་ལྟ་བུ་དང་པོ་དང་། སྒྲ་ཕལ་ཆེར་རྟག་ལས་ཆེ་སྙམ་པའི་ཡིད་གཉིས་ལྟ་བུ་གཉིས་པ་དང་། སྒྲ་རྟག་གམ་མི
རྟག་སྙམ་པའི་སེམས་ཉི་ལྟ་བུ་གསུམ་པ་ཡིན་པའི་ཕྱིར། །རང་གི་འཇུག་ཡུལ་དུ་གྱུར་པའི་རང་མཚན་གསལ་བར་སྣང་ཞིང་དེ་ལ་ངེས་པ་འདྲེན་མི་ནུས་པའི་རིག་པ། སྣང་ལ་མ་ངེས་པའི་བློའི་མཚན་ཉིད། དེ་ལ་དབྱེ་ན། དེར
གྱུར་པའི་དབང་མངོན། ཡིད་མངོན། རང་རིག་དང་གསུམ། དེར་གྱུར་པའི་རྣལ་འབྱོར་མངོན་སུམ་མེད་དེ། རྣལ་འབྱོར་མངོན་སུམ་ཡིན་ན་རང་ཡུལ་རྟོགས་པས་ཁྱབ་པའི་ཕྱིར་ཏེ། རྣམ་འགྲེལ་ལས། བློ་གྲོས་ཆེན་པོས་མཐོང་ཉིད

Tibetan Texts 5–12

ཁ ༄༅། ། ཕྱིར། རྣམ་པ་ཐམས་ཅད་ངེས་པར་བྱེད། ཅེས་གསུངས་པའི་ཕྱིར། མཚན་གཞི་ཡང་། ཤེལ་སྒོང་སྔོན་པོ་མཐོང་ངམ་མ་མཐོང་སྙམ་དུ་ཐེ་ཚོམ་འདྲེན་པར་བྱེད་པའི་སྔོ་འཛིན་དབང་མངོན་ལྟ་བུ་དང་པོ་དང་། སོ་སྐྱེའི་རྒྱུད་ཀྱི་
གཟུགས་འཛིན་ཡིད་མངོན་ལྟ་བུ་གཉིས་པ་དང་། རྒྱུད་འཕེལ་བའི་རྒྱུད་ཀྱི་རྗེས་དཔག་ཚད་མར་ཉམས་སུ་མྱོང་བའི་རང་རིག་ལྟ་བུ་གསུམ་པ་ཡིན་པའི་ཕྱིར་རོ། །༈ རང་གི་འཇུག་ཡུལ་ལ་འཁྲུལ་བའི་རིག་པ་ལོག་ཤེས་ཀྱི་མཚན་ཉིད། དེ་ལ་དབྱེ་
ན། རྟོག་པ་ལོག་ཤེས་དང་། རྟོག་མེད་ལོག་ཤེས་གཉིས། མཚན་གཞི་ནི། རི་བོང་རྭ་འཛིན་རྟོག་པ་དང་། གང་ཟག་གི་བདག་འཛིན་ལྟ་བུ་དང་པོ་དང་། གཉིས་པ་ལ་དབང་ཤེས་སུ་སྣང་བའི་དེ་དང་། ཡིད་ཤེས་སུ་སྣང་བའི་དེ་གཉིས་ལས་ཟླ་
བ་གཉིས་སྣང་གི་དབང་ཤེས་དང་གངས་རི་སྔོན་པོར་སྣང་བའི་དབང་ཤེས་ལྟ་བུ་དང་པོ་དང་། སྔོན་པོ་གསལ་བར་སྣང་བའི་རྨི་ལམ་གྱི་ཤེས་པ་ལྟ་བུ་གཉིས་པ་ཡིན་པའི་ཕྱིར། །༈ གཉིས་པ་བློ་རིག་གསུམ་དུ་དབྱེ་བ་ཡོད་དེ། དོན་སྤྱི་

བཟུང་ཡུལ་དུ་བྱེད་པའི་རྟོག་པ། རང་མཚན་བཟུང་ཡུལ་དུ་བྱེད་པའི་རྟོག་མེད་མ་འཁྲུལ་བའི་ཤེས་པ། མེད་པ་གསལ་སྣང་ཅན་བཟུང་ཡུལ་དུ་བྱེད་པའི་རྟོག་མེད་འཁྲུལ་ཤེས་དང་གསུམ་ཡོད་པའི་ཕྱིར། དང་པོ་དང་རྟོག་པ་གཉིས་
དོན་གཅིག །གཉིས་པ་དང་མངོན་སུམ་གཉིས་དོན་གཅིག །གསུམ་པ་དང་རྟོག་མེད་ལོག་ཤེས་གཉིས་དོན་གཅིག ༈ གསུམ་པ་བློ་རིག་གཉིས་སུ་དབྱེ་བ་ཡོད་དེ། ཚད་མ་དང་། ཚད་མིན་གྱི་ཤེས་པ་གཉིས་སུ་དབྱེ་བ། རྟོག་པ་དང་། རྟོག་
མེད་ཀྱི་ཤེས་པ་གཉིས་སུ་དབྱེ་བ། འཁྲུལ་ཤེས་དང་། མ་འཁྲུལ་བའི་ཤེས་པ་གཉིས་སུ་དབྱེ་བ། ཡིད་ཤེས་དང་། དབང་ཤེས་གཉིས་སུ་དབྱེ་བ། སེལ་འཇུག་གི་བློ་དང་། སྒྲུབ་འཇུག་གི་བློ་གཉིས་སུ་དབྱེ་བ། སེམས་དང་། སེམས་བྱུང་
གཉིས་སུ་དབྱེ་བ་རྣམས་སུ་ཡོད་པའི་ཕྱིར། དེ་རྣམས་སོ་སོའི་དོན་ཡང་། །༈ གསར་དུ་མི་བསླུ་བའི་རིག་པ་ཚད་མའི་མཚན་ཉིད། དབྱེ་ན། མངོན་སུམ་གྱི་ཚད་མ་དང་། རྗེས་སུ་དཔག་པའི་ཚད་མ་གཉིས། ཚད་མ་ལ་དེ་གཉིས་སུ་གྲངས་

ཁ ༄༅། ། ངེས་པ་ཡང་ཡིན་ཏེ། དེ་གཉིས་ལས་མང་ན་མི་དགོས་ཤིང་ཉུང་ན་མི་འདུ་བའི་ཕྱིར། འོན་ཀྱང་འདིའི་གྲངས་ངེས་ལོག་རྟོག་སེལ་བའི་གྲངས་ངེས་ཡིན་གྱི་ཕུང་སུམ་སེལ་བའི་གྲངས་ངེས་ནི་མ་ཡིན་ཏེ། ཚད་མ་
ཡིན་ན་དེ་གཉིས་གང་རུང་ཡིན་པས་མ་ཁྱབ་པའི་ཕྱིར་ཏེ། ཕྱིར་ཚད་མ་དེ་དེ་གཉིས་གང་རུང་དུ་འཇོག་དཀའ་བའི་ཕྱིར། དང་པོ་གྲུབ་སྟེ། ཕྱིར་ཚད་མའི་གྲངས་ལ་རྒྱང་འཕེན་པས་མངོན་སུམ་གཅིག་པུར་འདོད་པ་ནས། ཙ་རི་ཀ་པས་
བཅུ་གཅིག་ཏུ་འདོད་པའི་བར་གཞན་སྡེ་རྣམས་ཀྱིས་གྲངས་ལ་ལོག་པར་རྟོག་པ་དུ་མ་ཞིག་འབྱུང་བ་དེ་དགག་པའི་ཕྱིར་དུ་རིགས་པའི་དབང་ཕྱུག་གིས། གཞལ་བྱ་གཉིས་ཕྱིར་ཚད་མ་གཉིས་ཞེས་སོགས་དངོས་སྟོབས་ཀྱི་རིགས་པའི་
སྒོ་ནས་དེ་དག་ལེགས་པར་བཀག་ནས་ཚད་མ་ལ་དེ་གཉིས་སུ་གྲངས་ངེས་པར་བསྒྲུབ་པའི་ཕྱིར་རོ། །༈ ཡང་ཚད་མ་ལ་དབྱེ་ན། རང་ལས་ངེས་ཀྱི་ཚད་མ་དང་། གཞན་ལས་ངེས་ཀྱི་ཚད་མ་གཉིས། རང་གི་གཞལ་བྱའི་

བདག་ཉིད། མཐར་ཐུག་པ་ཡུལ་སྟེང་དུ་གནས་པ་མེད་པར་རང་ཉིད་མི་འབྱུང་བ་ལ་ངེས་པ་རང་སྟོབས་ཀྱིས་འདྲེན་ནུས་པའི་གསར་དུ་མི་བསླུ་བའི་རིག་པ་རང་ལས་ངེས་ཀྱི་ཚད་མའི་མཚན་ཉིད། དེ་འདྲེན་མི་ནུས་པར་ཕྱིས་འབྱུང་བསྐྱེད་
པའི་ཚད་མ་གཞན་ལ་བརྟེན་དགོས་པའི་གསར་དུ་མི་བསླུ་བའི་རིག་པ་གཞན་ལས་ངེས་ཀྱི་ཚད་མའི་མཚན་ཉིད། དང་པོ་ལ་དབྱེ་ན། དོན་གོམས་པ་ཅན་གྱི་དབང་མངོན་གྱི་ཚད་མ། དོན་བྱེད་སྣང་ཅན་གྱི་དབང་མངོན་གྱི་ཚད་མ། རང་རིག་
མངོན་སུམ་གྱི་ཚད་མ། རྣལ་འབྱོར་མངོན་སུམ་གྱི་ཚད་མ། རྗེས་སུ་དཔག་པའི་ཚད་མ་དང་ལྔ། མཚན་གཞི་ བུའི་རྒྱུད་ཀྱི་ཕའི་གཟུགས་འཛིན་པའི་དབང་མངོན་ལྟ་བུ་དང་པོ། མེ་བཙོ་སྲེག་གི་དོན་བྱེད་ནུས་པར་འཛིན་པའི་མེ་འཛིན་
དབང་མངོན་ལྟ་བུ་གཉིས་པ། ཚད་མ་ཉམས་སུ་མྱོང་བའི་རང་རིག་མངོན་སུམ་ལྟ་བུ་གསུམ་པ། གང་ཟག་གི་བདག་མེད་མངོན་སུམ་དུ་རྟོགས་པའི་ཡེ་ཤེས་ལྟ་བུ་བཞི་པ། སྒྲ་མི་རྟག་རྟོགས་ཀྱི་རྗེས་དཔག་ལྟ་བུ་ལྔ་པ་ཡིན་པའི་ཕྱིར།

༄༅། །དེ་ལྟར་ཡང་། རིགས་གཏེར་ལས། དོན་རིག་གཅིག་དང་རང་རིག་གཅིག །རྗེས་སུ་དཔག་རྣམས་རང་ལས་ངེས། ཞེས་པའི་དགོངས་པ་ནི། །གཉིས་པ་གཞན་ལས་ངེས་ཀྱི་ཚད་མ་ལ་སྤྲུལ་བརྗོད་རིགས་ཀྱི་སྒོ་ནས་དབྱེ་ན། སྣང་
བ་རང་ལས་ངེས་ཤིང་འདྲེན་པ་གཞན་ལས་ངེས་པ། ཕྱིར་རང་ལས་ངེས་ཤིང་ཁྱད་པར་གཞན་ལས་ངེས་པ། སྣང་བ་ཉིད་ཀྱང་གཞན་ལས་ངེས་པ་དང་གསུམ། མཚན་གཞི་ནི། དོན་ལ་མེ་རི་ཁ་དོག་ཡིན་ཞིང་ཏོག་པས་མེ་རི་ཁ་དོག་ཡིན་མིན
ཐེ་ཚོམ་ཟ་དུས་ཀྱི་རྒྱུད་རིང་པོའི་ཁ་དོག་དམར་ལམ་པ་འཛིན་པའི་དབང་མངོན་ལྟ་བུ་དང་པོ་དང་། དོན་ལ་མེ་པ་ཡིན་ཞིང་ཏོག་པས་མེ་པ་ཡིན་མིན་ཐེ་ཚོམ་ཟ་དུས་ཀྱི་རྒྱུད་རིང་པོའི་ཤིང་འཛིན་དབང་མངོན་ལྟ་བུ་གཉིས་པ་དང་།
ཁོ་བོས་སྔོན་པོ་མཐོང་དམ་མ་མཐོང་སྙམ་པའི་ཐེ་ཚོམ་འདྲེན་པར་བྱེད་པའི་སྔོ་འཛིན་དབང་མངོན་ལྟ་བུ་གསུམ་པ་ཡིན། དེ་ཡང་དང་པོ་གཉིས་དངོས་ནི། ཐམས་པ་ཏུ་ཀས་པ་པར་འཛིན། །ཡང་དེ་ལ་རྣམ་རིང་གི་སྒོ་ནས

ཕྱེ་ན། མངོན་སུམ་དང་པོ་བ། ཡིད་མ་གཏད། འཁྲུལ་རྒྱུ་ཅན་དང་གསུམ་ཡང་ཡོད་དེ། རིགས་གཏེར་ལས། དང་པོ་བ་དང་ཡིད་མ་གཏད། འཁྲུལ་རྒྱུ་ཅན་རྣམས་གཞན་ལས་ངེས། ཞེས་གསུངས་པའི་ཕྱིར། དེ་རྣམས་ཀྱི
མཚན་གཞི་ཡང་ཡོད་དེ། སྔར་ཨུཏྤལ་མཐོང་མ་མྱོང་བའི་སྐྱེས་བུའི་རྒྱུད་ཀྱི་ཨུཏྤལ་གྱི་ཁ་དོག་འཛིན་པའི་དབང་མངོན་ལྟ་བུ་དང་པོ་དང་། ཡིད་གཟུགས་མཛེས་ལ་ལྷག་པར་ཆགས་དུས་ཀྱི་སྐྱེས་བུའི་རྒྱུད་ཀྱི་སྒྲ་འཛིན
དབང་མངོན་ལྟ་བུ་གཉིས་པ་དང་། སྨིག་རྒྱུ་ལ་ཆུ་འཛིན་གྱི་བློ་འདྲེན་དངོས་སུ་སྐྱེས་པའི་སྨིག་རྒྱུའི་ཁ་དོག་འཛིན་པའི་དབང་མངོན་ལྟ་བུ་གསུམ་པ་ཡིན་པའི་ཕྱིར། །༈ གསར་དུ་མི་སླུ་བ་མ་ཡིན་པའི་རིག་པ་ཚད་མིན
གྱི་ཤེས་པའི་མཚན་ཉིད། དབྱེ་བ་བཅད་ཤེས་སོགས་བློ་རིགས་ཕྱི་མ་ལྔའོ། །༈ སྒྲ་དོན་འདྲེས་རུང་དུ་འཛིན་པའི་ཞེན་རིག་རྟོག་པའི་མཚན་ཉིད། དེ་དང་སེལ་འཇུག་གི་བློ་གཉིས་དོན་གཅིག །མཚན་གཞི། རྗེས་དཔག །

༄༅། །ཡིད་དཔྱོད། ཐེ་ཚོམ་གསུམ་དང་། བཅད་ཤེས་ལོག་ཤེས་གཉིས་ཀྱི་ཕྱོགས་གཅིག་རྣམས་འཛོམ། །༈ སྒྲ་དོན་འདྲེས་རུང་དུ་འཛིན་པའི་ཞེན་རིག་དང་བྲལ་བའི་རིག་པ་རྟོག་མེད་ཀྱི་ཤེས་པའི་མཚན་ཉིད། དེ་དང
སྒྲུབ་འཇུག་གི་བློ་གཉིས་དོན་གཅིག །མཚན་གཞི། མངོན་སུམ། སྣང་ལ་མ་ངེས་པའི་བློ་གཉིས་དང་། བཅད་ཤེས་ལོག་ཤེས་གཉིས་ཀྱི་ཕྱོགས་གཅིག་རྣམས་འཛོམ། །༈ རང་གི་སྣང་ཡུལ་ལ་འཁྲུལ་བའི་རིག་པ་འཁྲུལ་ཤེས
ཀྱི་མཚན་ཉིད། མཚན་གཞི། ལོག་ཤེས་དང་རྟོག་པ་ཐམས་ཅད་དོ། །༈ རང་གི་སྣང་ཡུལ་ལ་མ་འཁྲུལ་བའི་རིག་པ་མ་འཁྲུལ་བའི་ཤེས་པའི་མཚན་ཉིད། དེ་དང་མངོན་སུམ་གཉིས་དོན་གཅིག །དེ་ཡང་མདོ་སྡེ་པའི་དབང་དུ་བྱས
ཀྱི་ཉམས་རིག་པའི་ལུགས་ལ་དེ་ལྟར་ཡིན་ཏེ། མངོན་སུམ་ལ་འཁྲུལ་མ་འཁྲུལ་གྱི་ཆ་གཉིས་སུ་འདོད་པའི་ཕྱིར། །༈ རང་གི་ཐུན་མོང་མ་ཡིན་པའི་བདག་རྐྱེན་ཡིད་དབང་ལ་བརྟེན་ནས་སྐྱེས་པའི་རིག་པ་ཡིད་ཤེས་ཀྱི་མཚན

ཉིད། ཡིད་དང་། ཡིད་ཤེས་ལ་མུ་བཞི། དང་པོ་ཡིན་ལ་ཕྱི་མ་མིན་པ། མིག་གི་རྣམ་ཤེས་ལྟ་བུ། ཕྱི་མ་ཡིན་ལ། དང་པོ་མིན་པ། ཡིད་ཤེས་འཁོར་གྱི་སེམས་བྱུང་ཐམས་ཅད། གཉིས་ཀ་ཡིན་པ། ཡིད་ཀྱི་རྣམ་པར་ཤེས་པ།
གཉིས་ཀ་མིན་པ་དབང་ཤེས་འཁོར་གྱི་སེམས་བྱུང་ཐམས་ཅད་དོ། །དེ་བཞིན་དུ། བུམ་འཛིན་རྟོག་པ་དང་། བུམ་པ་རྟོགས་པའི་རྟོག་པ་ལ་མུ་བཞི། ཆོས་དེ་ལ་མངོན་སུམ་དང་། ཆོས་དེ་ལ་མངོན་སུམ་ཚད་མ་གཉིས་ལ་མུ
བཞི། ཆོས་དེ་ལ་རྗེས་དཔག་ཚད་མ་དང་། ཆོས་དེ་ལ་རྟོག་པ་གཉིས་ལ་མུ་བཞི། དེའི་རྟགས་ལས་རྟོགས་པ་དང་། དེའི་རྟགས་ཀྱིས་རྟོགས་པ་ལ་ཁྱད་པར་ཡོད་ཅིང་། ཡུལ་དེ་མངོན་སུམ་གྱིས་རྟོགས་པ་དང་། མངོན་སུམ་
དུ་རྟོགས་པ་ལ་ཁྱད་པར་ཡོད་ཚུལ་རྣམས་ཁྱད་པར་ཕྱེ་ནས་ཤེས་དགོས་ཏེ། པཎ་ཆེན་ཉིད་ཀྱིས་མདོ་ཆད་པའི་རྣམས་ལ་གཅེས་པར་བྱུང་ངོ་ཞིག །ཅེས་གསུངས་པའི་ཕྱིར། །༈ རང་གི་ཐུན་མོང་མ་ཡིན་པའི

Tibetan Texts 13–20

ཀ། ༄༅། །བདག་རྐྱེན་དབང་པོ་གཟུགས་ཅན་པ་ལ་བརྟེན་ནས་སྐྱེས་པའི་རིག་པ་དབང་ཤེས་ཀྱི་མཚན་ཉིད། དབྱེ་ན། མིག་ཤེས། རྣ་ཤེས། སྣ་ཤེས། ལྕེ་ཤེས། ལུས་ཤེས་དང་ལྔ། །༄ རང་ཡུལ་ལ་ཞེན་དབང་གིས་
འཇུག་པའི་རིག་པ་སེལ་འཇུག་གི་བློའི་མཚན་ཉིད། དེ་དང་རྟོག་པ་གཉིས་དོན་གཅིག །༄ རང་ཡུལ་ལ་དངོས་དབང་གིས་འཇུག་པའི་རིག་པ་སྒྲུབ་འཇུག་གི་བློའི་མཚན་ཉིད། དེ་དང་རྟོག་མེད་ཀྱི་ཤེས་པ་གཉིས་དོན་གཅིག
༄ རང་གི་འཁོར་དུ་བྱུང་བའི་སེམས་བྱུང་དང་མཚུངས་པར་ལྡན་པ་སེམས་ཀྱི་མཚན་ཉིད། སེམས་དང་། ཡིད་དང་། རྣམ་ཤེས་གསུམ་དོན་གཅིག །༄ རང་འཁོར་དུ་ལྡན་པའི་སེམས་དང་མཚུངས་པར་ལྡན་པ་སེམས་བྱུང་
གི་མཚན་ཉིད། མཚུངས་ལྡན་ལྔ་ཚུལ་ཡོད་དེ། དཔེར་ན་མིག་གི་རྣམ་ཤེས་དང་། དེའི་འཁོར་གྱི་ཚོར་བ་གཉིས་ལྟ་བུ། དམིགས་པ་གཅིག་པས་དམིགས་པ་མཚུངས། །འཛིན་སྟངས་གཅིག་པས་རྣམ་པ་མཚུངས། །དུས་གཅིག

པས་དུས་མཚུངས། ཐུན་མོང་མ་ཡིན་པའི་བདག་རྐྱེན་གཅིག་པས་རྟེན་མཚུངས། །མིག་གི་རྣམ་ཤེས་རྫས་རེ་རེའི་འཁོར་དུ་ཚོར་བ་ཡང་རྫས་རེ་རེ་བོ་ན་འབྱུང་བས་རྫས་མཚུངས་པ་སྟེ་མཚུངས་ལྡན་རྣམ་པ་ལྔ་མཚུངས་ཡིན་ནོ།།
མཚན་ཉིད་དེ་དག་གི་ངོ་བོ་གཙོ་བོར་བྱས་ཀྱི་ཆོས་སྤྱི་གཅོད་པ་གཙོ་བོར་བྱེད་ན་མཚན་ཉིད་གང་ལ་རང་སྟོབས་ཐོག་ནས་ཡོད་ཅེ་མཚོན་བྱ་ལ་ཡང་དེ་རང་ཉིད་དེ་ཡིན་པའི་ཞེས་སྦྱར་དགོས་སོ། །སེམས་བྱུང་ལ་དབྱེ་ན་རྩ་ཚན་དྲུག
ཡོད་དེ། ཀུན་འགྲོ་ལྔ་དང་ཡུལ་ངེས་ལྔ། །དགེ་བ་བཅུ་གཅིག་རྩ་ཉོན་དྲུག །ཉེ་ཉོན་ཉི་ཤུ་གཞན་འགྱུར་བཞི། །སེམས་བྱུང་ང་གཅིག་འདི་དག་གོ །ཚོར་བ་འདུ་ཤེས་སེམས་པ་དང་། །ཡིད་ལ་བྱེད་དང་རེག་པ་ལྔ། །གཙོ
སེམས་ཀུན་གྱི་འཁོར་དུ་ནི། །འགྲོ་ཕྱིར་ཀུན་འགྲོ་ཞེས་བྱའོ། །འདུན་པ་མོས་པ་དྲན་པ་དང་། །ཏིང་འཛིན་ཤེས་རབ་ལྔ་པོ་ཡུལ། །བྱེ་བྲག་པ་ལ་འཇུག་ངེས་ཕྱིར། །ཡུལ་ངེས་ཞེས་སུ་བཤད་པ་ཡིན། །དད་དང་ངོ་

ཀ། ༄༅། །ཚ་ཤེས་ཁྲེལ་ཡོད། །འདོད་ཆགས་དང་ནི་ཞེ་སྡང་དང་། །གཏི་མུག་མེད་པའི་དགེ་རྩ་གསུམ། །བརྩོན་འགྲུས་ཤིན་སྦྱངས་བག་ཡོད་དང་། །བཏང་སྙོམས་རྣམ་པར་མི་འཚེ་རྣམས། །གཉེན་པ་ངོ་བོ
མཚུངས་ལྡན་སོགས། །ཅི་རིགས་སྒོ་ནས་དགེ་བའོ། །འདོད་ཆགས་ཁོང་ཁྲོ་ང་རྒྱལ་དང་། །མ་རིག་ཐེ་ཚོམ་ལྟ་བ་དྲུག །འདི་གསུམ་ཉོན་མོངས་ཅན་ཞེས་བྱ། །རྩ་ཉོན་ཡིན་ཏེ་སེམས་རྒྱུད་ནི། །ཉོན་མོངས་བྱེད་པའི་གཙོ་བོ་འོ།།
ཁྲོ་བ་འཁོན་འཛིན་འཆབ་དང་ཚིག །ཕྲག་དོག་སེར་སྣ་སྒྱུ་དང་གཡོ། །རྒྱགས་དང་རྣམ་འཚེ་ངོ་ཚ་མེད། །ཁྲེལ་མེད་རྨུགས་རྒོད་མ་དད་པ། །ལེ་ལོ་བག་མེད་བརྗེད་ངེས་དང་། །ཤེས་བཞིན་མ་ཡིན་རྣམ་གཡེང་བཅས། །ཉི་ཤུ
རྩ་ཉོན་ལ་བརྟེན་སྐྱེས་དང་། །ཉེ་ཕྱིར་ཉེ་བའི་ཉོན་མོངས་སོ། །གཉིད་འགྱོད་རྟོག་དཔྱོད་གཞན་འགྱུར་ཏེ། །ཀུན་སློང་མཚུངས་ལྡན་ཅི་རིགས་ཀྱིས། །དགེ་དང་མི་དགེ་ལུང་མ་བསྟན། །གཞན་དང་གཞན་དུ་འགྱུར་བའོ། །

དེ་དག་སོ་སོའི་ངོ་བོ་དང་། །བྱེད་ལས་རྒྱས་བཤད་གཞུང་མང་སོར། །བློ་ལྡན་རྣམས་ཀྱིས་ཤེས་འདོད་ན། །ཞིབ་ཏུ་མངོན་པའི་གཞུང་ལས་ཤེས། །ཉེས་ཚོར་མཆིས་ན་མཁས་ལ་བཤགས། །དགེ་བ་བདག་འདྲའི་བློ་དམན་གྱི། །
མོངས་པ་སེལ་བར་བྱེད་པའི་མཐུས། །རྒྱལ་བསྟན་ཡུན་དུ་གནས་གྱུར་ཅིག །ཅེས་བློ་རིག་གི་རྣམ་བཞག་ཉེར་མཁོ་ཀུན་བཏུས་འདི་འདྲ་ཞིག་བློ་གླིང་དཔེ་མཛོད་པ་ཨ་ཁུ་ཀུན་གྱིས་ཡང་ཡང་བསྐུལ་བ་ལ་བརྟེན། ཉ་སྟོད་བློ་རིག་ལ་གཞི་མ་བྱས། པཎ་ཆེན
གྱི་ཡིག་ཆ་རང་ལ་བ་རྣམས་རྗེ་བཞིན་དུ་བཀོད། དེར་མི་གསལ་བ་མཚན་ཉིད་སོགས་འགའ་ཞིག་བསྡུར་ནས་རྣམས་བློ་རིག་ཐོམ་དང་ཡོངས་འཛིན་བློ་རིག་གཉིས་དང་ཅི་རིགས་སུ་མཐུན་པར་སྦྱར་བ་འདི་ནི། སྟོད་གླིང་སློབ་དཔོན་ཁྲི་ཐོག་པ་རྒྱལ་རོང་དགེ་བཤེས་སྒྱུར་
དཔོན་བཟང་མ་དཔལ་བ་མ་འཕེལ་ནས་གཞན་ཕན་ཀྱི་ཡང་ཞོལ་དུ་བྱུར་བ་འདི་ལ་བཀྲ་ཤིས་མ་པ་ཤེས་གཉེན་ཡོངས་ཀྱི་ཚོ་མཐུན་དུ་གྱུར་པ་དགེ་ལེགས་འཕེལ།། ༄ སྒྲ་ཚུལ། ངག་དང་ཨ་ངག་སྤྱོད་བཅུད་འཛིན་ཆེན་དང་། །སྒྲིད་བཞིན་

ཁྲ། ༄༅། །བཅིངས་དང་གྲོལ་བའི་བྱེད་པོ་ཉིད། །ཀུན་བྱུང་སྙིང་འམ་སེམས་འདི་ཡིན་ཚུལ་ལ། །རྒྱལ་དང་བཅས་སྲས་ཀུན་གྱིས་མཁྱེན་གཅིག་ཏུ། །ཡིད་ཆེས་ལུང་ལས་ཡང་ཡང་གསུངས་པའི་དོན། །ཐོག་མར་ཐོས་
བྱུང་ཡིད་དཔྱོད་གོ་བ་བཙལ། །ཡང་དག་རིགས་པའི་སྒོ་ནས་བསམ་བྱུང་གི །རྗེས་སུ་དཔག་པས་སྣང་ལམ་ངེས་དང་། །ཐེ་ཚོམ་ལོག་རྟོག་སྒྲོ་འདོགས་ཀུན་ཆོད་ནས། །བཅད་དོན་ཐོབ་པའི་ངེས་ཤེས་རྒྱུད་དུ་སྐྱེས། །
དེ་ལྟར་གོམས་པས་གསལ་སྣང་སྒོམ་བྱུང་གི །མྱོང་བ་ཐོབ་པའི་རྣལ་འབྱོར་མངོན་སུམ་གྱི། །གོམས་པ་མཐར་ཕྱིན་ཀུན་མཁྱེན་ཡེ་ཤེས་ཐོབ། །ཚུལ་འདིར་བློ་ལྡན་རྣམས་ཀྱིས་གཅེས་པར་མཛོད། །དད་སྟོབས་ལྷ་
ལམ་ཡངས་པའི་འཇམ་སྦྱིན་ནས། །པར་བསྐྲུན་ལེགས་བྱས་རྣམ་དཀར་རབ་སེལ་ཟེར་གྱིས། །དུཿཁ་བསམ་ཚོགས་གདུང་སྡོང་སྨན་ཀུན་བསལ་ནས། །རྣམ་དཔྱོད་ཀུ་མུད་ཀ་ཡི་འདབ་བརྒྱ་གྲོལ། །མཐུར་འགྲོ་ཀུན་བདེ་

གཉེན་དེད་དཔོན་གྱིས། །ཐོས་བསམ་སྒོམ་པའི་གྲུ་གཟིངས་བརྩོན་འགྲུས་ཀྱི། །མཐུན་པའི་བསེར་བུས་ཉེ་བར་རབ་བསྐུལ་ནས། །གླིང་མཆོག་སྨྲ་ཏེ་ཐར་པའི་གླིང་དུ་འགོད། །རྒྱལ་བའི་བསྟན་པ་ཕྱོགས་བཅུར་དར་ཞིང་
རྒྱས། །རྒྱལ་དབང་མཆོག་གི་ཞབས་ཟུང་བསྐལ་བརྒྱར་བརྟན། །རྒྱལ་དང་ཆོས་ཀྱི་སྲིད་བྱུང་མདའ་ཐང་རྒྱས། །རྒྱལ་ཁམས་དགའ་བདེའི་དཔལ་ལ་རྟག་རོལ་ཤོག །ཅེས་པར་བྱང་གི་སྨོན་ཚིག་འདི་ཡང་པར་བསྐྲུན་
ལྷ་སྦྱོར་བ་འབྲས་རྒྱས་པ་ཧ་ཐུར་འཇམ་དབྱངས་སྦྱིན་པ་ནས་བསྐུལ་བ་ངོར་གོང་གི་ཚོམ་པ་པོས་མཚམས་སྦྱར་ནས་བྲིས་པའོ།། ཞེ་སོག་བདེ་བཞིན་ནམ་མཁའ་སྦྱོར་བ་ཉེར་བའི་ཚེད་གྲངས་ཟླ་བ་ཚང་གཞུང་ནས་ཡོན་སྦྱར་
ཏེ་པར་བསྐྲུན་ཞུས་པའོ།། སརྦ་མངྒ་ལཾ།། ||

Tibetan Texts 21–26

Errata

page and line	*mistake*	*correction*
38.6	ser sna	ser sna)
46.26	clear and knowing'.]	clear and knowing'.
60.7	bzung ba	bzung ba)
69.36	uncontradictible	uncontradictable
72.22	arise from	arisen from
74.12	seven fold	sevenfold
78.21	atyartha	(atyartha
78.21	gyur)	gyur).
92.4	it adheres one-pointedly	it determines one-pointedly
99, last line	object of operation	object of engagement
100.4	discerned object	determined object
101.1	object of operation	object of engagement
109.13	object of operation	object of engagement